BLAZE YOUR OWN TRAIL

IDEAS FOR TEENS TO FIND AND PURSUE YOUR PURPOSE

Justin Ashley
art by Cory Thomas

free spirit
PUBLISHING®

Library of Congress Cataloging-in-Publication Data
Names: Ashley, Justin, 1985– author. | Thomas, Cory, artist.
Title: Blaze your own trail : ideas for teens to find and pursue your purpose / Justin Ashley ; art by Cory Thomas.
Description: Minneapolis, MN : Free Spirit Publishing, an imprint of Teacher Created Materials, [2024] | Includes index. | Audience: Ages 13+
Identifiers: LCCN 2023003404 (print) | LCCN 2023003405 (ebook) | ISBN 9781631987281 (paperback) | ISBN 9781631987298 (ebook) | ISBN 9781631987304 (epub)
Subjects: LCSH: Self-actualization (Psychology) in adolescence—Juvenile literature. | Self-efficacy—Juvenile literature. | Goal (Psychology)—Juvenile literature. | BISAC: YOUNG ADULT NONFICTION / Inspirational & Personal Growth | YOUNG ADULT NONFICTION / Social Topics / Self-Esteem & Self-Reliance
Classification: LCC BF724.3.S25 A84 2023 (print) | LCC BF724.3.S25 (ebook) | DDC 155.4/19—dc23/eng/20230207
LC record available at https://lccn.loc.gov/2023003404
LC ebook record available at https://lccn.loc.gov/2023003405

Edited by Alison Behnke
Cover and interior design by Courtenay Fletcher
Illustrated by Cory Thomas

Printed in China

Free Spirit Publishing
An imprint of Teacher Created Materials
9850 51st Avenue North, Suite 100
Minneapolis, MN 55442
(612) 338-2068
help4kids@freespirit.com
freespirit.com

FSC
www.fsc.org
MIX
Paper | Supporting responsible forestry
FSC® C144853

To my two favorite trailblazers,
Cole and Savannah Ashley.
–J.A.

To everyone who believes in me.
Thanks from your invisible friend.
–C.T.

CONTENTS

Part Three: THE ONWARD PATH

You must learn one thing.
The world was made to be free in.

Give up all the other worlds
except the one to which you belong.

Sometimes it takes darkness and the sweet
confinement of your aloneness
to learn

anything or anyone
that does not bring you alive

is too small for you.
　　　—David Whyte

INTRODUCTION

I was a weird kid.

For example, my favorite food on earth? Biscuits and ketchup. It was cute and funny at four years old but kind of strange when I was still eating it at 12. By this time, there was a part of me that was embarrassed by my preference. Shouldn't I just be normal and eat a plain biscuit (or one covered with gravy or jelly) like everyone else?

The answer to that question came to me on my 13th birthday. My family had planned a big party at my grandparents' house. They sat me down at the dining room table by the kitchen, surrounded by my aunts, uncles, cousins, sister, and grandfather.

Out of the corner of my eye, I saw my grandmother sneaking in from the kitchen. She held a plate of 13 crisp, golden biscuits in one hand, hot out of the oven, each one crowned with a lit candle. In her other hand, she held a brand-new bottle of ketchup.

She stood behind me as the family choir began singing "Happy Birthday." I looked up at her and, to this day, still remember her warm smile and gentle eyes, sending me a clear and glorious message: "Embrace your weirdness. Don't be normal. Be you." In that rite of passage from childhood to adolescence—just when I was about to conform—my grandmother loved me, adored me, and celebrated me in a way no other person in my life ever has.

I've been living the weird life ever since. I might seem to be a strange mix of apparent contradictions to others, but to me it all just feels right. I was raised in a Baptist church, and I also practice Buddhist meditation and study Stoic philosophy. I have a cross tattoo on my arm and work summers at the local Jewish community center. I was born and raised in the South, and still live there, but I also thrive on meeting people across the country—and around the world. In my free time, I enjoy reading about Bigfoot, the Loch Ness Monster, and UFOs. I love walking in nature alone, and also playing team sports like basketball and football. I'm a macho man who has a mental illness and isn't ashamed to talk about it openly. I'm a teacher who cares at *least* as much about my students having fun while they learn as I do about the scores they get on an end-of-year exam.

Some kids start life strange and lose that uniqueness as they get older. Society conditions them to be more "normal." Me? I've only become stranger with age.

I have my grandmother to thank for that. She provided me with a unique birthday gift, giving me the courage to forge ahead and blaze my own trail. And above all, she taught me *self-acceptance*. What I've learned over time is that sometimes you will have approval and support from loved ones around you, and other times, they won't celebrate you the way you wish for. It's in these moments, most of all, that you'll need to accept and celebrate yourself.

ARE YOU WEIRD?

How about you? Are you weird?

Are you obsessed with '90s grunge when all your friends only listen to the latest hits? Do you like to dye your hair purple or rock an '80s mullet? Are you the only person who laughs at your jokes? Does it feel like no one in your school—or even your town—shares your political views? Are you deeply spiritual even though no one else in your family believes in God? Do you question the existence of a higher power even though your family attends worship every week? When you look in the mirror, do you feel like you're too tall or too short?

Or, even if none of these exact questions resonates with you, do you ever just feel like an outsider?

If so, the pages that follow are for you. This isn't a warm, fuzzy book about loving yourself. It's about creating and owning your own weird, wonderful path and embracing it with your whole spirit. It's not about following somebody else, but about leading yourself all the way to a destination *you* define, even when others call for you to turn back and follow the beaten path.

THE THREE PATHS

If you are committed to this process of forging your unique path, you can become a trailblazer by taking three simultaneous journeys, which make up the three sections of this book:

1. **THE INNER PATH:** This section is about interpretation. You'll learn how to create a fresh vision for your future, translate the dreams that come to you at night, use technology for good, regulate your emotions using ancient Stoic wisdom, breathe through your fears, connect with nature through techniques such as *earthing*, protect

yourself from becoming a Zombie Student, and use your unique personal values as a compass to move forward.

2. **THE OUTER PATH:** This section is about connection. You'll set up a Teen Squad, figure out how to benefit from negative feedback without being so hard on yourself, intersect your path with friends and family by going on mini-adventures together, create a sanctuary for studying, practice a Danish concept called hygge, honor the heroes in your story, and exercise the Stoic principle of amor fati to find gratitude in any environment along your path.

3. **THE ONWARD PATH:** This section is about determination. You'll explore ways to incorporate more movement into your life, reach back and revive a few simple joys from your childhood, create (and follow) plans for school days as well as your time off, strengthen your mental fortitude based on the theory of multiple intelligences, learn to communicate from your head and your heart, have courageous conversations with anxiety, and help yourself heal if you experience depression.

HOW TO USE THIS BOOK

You can read this book as a free spirit—from beginning to end, end to beginning, or by flipping to the chapters that may resonate with you in the moment.

For example, if you are fearful about something that may happen in your future, chapter 5 ("Stare into the Snake") could be helpful. Or if you are struggling with friendships, you could read chapter 9, which is all about creating a Teen Squad. You could even page through the book simply reading chapters with artwork that really catches your eye. The main idea is this: I want you to feel free to pick this book up, put it down, and come back to it when you desire.

Whichever way you choose to proceed with this book—and with your trailblazing mission—I know this is no easy road. I applaud you for taking this path. And I also want to let you know up front that I can't be your leader. Only you can.

However, if you're ready to blaze your trail, it will help to have a mentor with a little trailblazing experience of their own. I'll do my best to be that for you—not to define your path for you, but to prepare, equip, and nudge you in the direction that calls to you. Not to give you all the answers, but to offer you ideas and support. To bring light to the traveler's spirit that may still be in darkness or lying dormant within you.

CARVING YOUR PATH

It probably won't surprise you that a lot of people—including a lot of teens—deal with mental health issues like anxiety, depression, and suicidal thoughts. You may have faced such challenges yourself. I know I have. One reason for this may be nihilism, the belief that life has little or no meaning.

Plenty of teens see the path their teachers, parents, and community have laid out for them: attend school, get married, have kids, work for decades, retire (if they're lucky), and die. They might think to themselves, *This is it? This is what life is all about? What's the point? I don't want to play the game. I quit.*

If this is where you're at right now, it's not a bad starting point, believe it or not. We can begin here, but this isn't how it has to end. If you don't like the plans laid out for you, create your own. Map out a new path, using your values, vision, and purpose. There is so much joy and adventure in the path of self-discovery you are about to take.

In the words of the German philosopher Friedrich Nietzsche, "No one can build you the bridge on which you, and only you, must cross the river of life. There may be countless trails and bridges and demigods who would gladly carry you across; but only at the price of pawning and forgoing yourself. There is one path in the world that none can walk but you. Where does it lead? Don't ask, walk!"

It's time for us to start walking. Not yet outward, nor onward—but first, within.

I can't wait to hear what you think of this book, and if the ideas in it worked for you—or if you have ideas of your own to add. If you'd like to share your thoughts with me, please email me at justinfashley@gmail.com, message or tag me on Instagram @justinashley, or write to me at:

Teacher Created Materials
P.O. Box 1040
Huntington Beach, CA 92647

PART ONE
THE INNER PATH

CHAPTER 1

CREATE A VISION BOARD TO TEXT THE UNIVERSE YOUR DREAMS

Harper Grace.

You might not know her name, but for a while, a whole lot of people did—for all the wrong reasons. When she was just 11 years old, Harper sang the national anthem at a Major League Soccer game in front of over 20,000 fans.

If you've never seen the video, be warned—it's challenging to watch. To put it mildly, Harper struggled through the song. Almost immediately after her performance ended, it went viral on news outlets and social media. People were calling it one of the worst performances of the song in history.

Can you imagine what that must have felt like for Harper? She was a young girl with big dreams who fell short in her significant moment and was then publicly shamed. I wonder if, when she went out, people recognized her, pointed, and laughed. That was likely a rock-bottom time for her, and she probably spent some time feeling sorry for herself. It's only natural. But rather than *continue* to meditate on her failure, she decided to focus on the future. As she explained it, "I created this dream board. It has all the things that I want to accomplish when I'm older."

All around the board, she placed printed pictures and magazine cut-outs of guitars, pianos, music notes, people she wanted to help, and places she wanted to go. In the center she put a list of things she wanted to accomplish. One of those things was to try out for *American Idol* and "maybe win."

In 2018 she got her chance. She sang two songs in front of Katy Perry, Lionel Richie, and Luke Bryan. With a guitar in hand, she played an original song called "Yard Sale." She also performed Khalid's "Young Dumb & Broke." And she crushed it! She received substantial compliments from each judge for her songwriting and vocals.

At the end of Harper's performance, Katy Perry asked to see her dream board, which she'd brought with her to the audition room. Katy took her pen, crossed out "maybe," and wrote, "Going to Hollywood." Luke Bryan handed her the golden ticket, and Harper made it to the Top 50, out of thousands of contestants. Redemption!

REPLACE SHAME WITH SELF-COMPASSION

Have you ever experienced failure like Harper did at that game—even if your audience wasn't as big? Have you felt so locked up in a past mistake that you couldn't think about anything else or you felt like a total failure every time it came to mind? It might sound like this:

- *"I bombed that math test. I'm so stupid."*
- *"I tried to talk to them, and they didn't even respond to my text. I'm such a loser."*
- *"I lied to my mom, and she'll never look at me the same. I'm a bad kid."*

These kinds of thoughts all come from a singular source: *shame*. Shame says, "I'm a bad singer. I'm a bad student. I'm a bad athlete. I'm a bad friend. I'm a bad person." Shame is destructive and can keep you stuck in the past. On the other hand, *self-compassion* offers a way forward after you've been through something hard. It gives you tools for the future, because it doesn't suggest you are bad in nature—only that you had a bad performance.

Shame is a critical inner voice. At a fundamental level, it's the belief that you aren't enough—whether because of a mistake, or a series of mistakes, or simply because of some core aspect of yourself. This voice can become so loud and so intense that it overpowers your identity, casting a shadow over your past, present, and future. But with self-compassion, difficult experiences become opportunities to give yourself grace (pun intended) in the present and ultimately catapult you into a better future.

What does self-compassion sound like? Here are some examples:

- *"My shots were off this game, but my form is good and I believe I'll have a better game next week."*

- *"While this friendship didn't work out, I know my worth doesn't come from getting others to accept me. I earn my worth by being my true, authentic self. Those who love my vibe will connect with me. Those who don't, well—they don't need to be part of my life."*
- *"I didn't understand a lot of the content in this unit, but my intelligence isn't determined by one failed test. I'm a smart person with a strong work ethic."*
- *"I hit the wrong notes today, but I have a beautiful voice and will continue singing."*

Harper may have initially felt shame after failing to perform the anthem in a way she knew she could, but she didn't get stuck there. She accepted the event as part of her past, turned her attention to what lay ahead, and worked hard. And that's why she earned that golden ticket to Hollywood.

One way to work with a feeling of failure or mediocrity is to do precisely what Harper did and create a dream board, also referred to as a vision board. Why is this important? For one, it shifts your mindset from the past tense to the present and future tenses. This shift is essential, because the truth is that you have zero control over what's already happened. Your power and your energy—even if they're still dormant—lie in the present. Now it's up to you to awaken them, though inspiration and imagination. By creating strong mental, visual, and tangible images of what you desire in the months and years to come, you are waking up that present energy and moving forward with clarity.

Here are some ideas for how to start.

1. **BEGIN WITH A BRAINSTORM.** Whether on paper, on a computer or tablet, or on your phone, write answers to these 11 questions:
   - What kind of person do you want to be?
   - What do you want to do for fun?

- What story do you want your life to tell?
- What kinds of feelings do you want to have?
- What do you want to feel spiritually?
- What types of people do you want in your life, both now and in the future?
- What do you want to accomplish in school, sports, or elsewhere?
- Do you want to go to college? If so, do you know what school (or schools) you hope to attend?
- What job or career do you aspire to have?
- What kind of life do you want to have financially? What material things do you want?
- How could you support philanthropies or charitable causes you care about—or maybe one day even create a fundraiser or nonprofit organization of your own?

2. **COLLECT YOUR MATERIALS.** You'll only need a few:
   - a bulletin board or a piece of poster board
   - markers and colored pencils
   - an assortment of pictures you've collected from magazines, online, or elsewhere
   - inspirational quote cards with phrases like "We rise by lifting others" and "You were born an original. Don't die a copy." (You can order these online or make your own.)
   - tape or glue

3. **BUILD YOUR VISION BOARD.** Use your answers to the brainstorm questions and your materials to put your vision board together. You can see a sample idea on the next page. If you'd like to use

a template, you can download one at go.freespirit.com/blaze or from the "free stuff" section of my website, justinfashley.com. And have fun! The process of making this board should be creative and exciting as you think about all your ideas for the future.

4. **PLACE YOUR BOARD IN A HIGHLY VISIBLE LOCATION.** You've likely heard the expression, "out of sight, out of mind." The opposite is also true. If something is highly visible, you're going to be reminded of it regularly. It's not magic. It's magnetic. You're sending out messages—texting your thoughts, dreams, and desires into the universe. Eventually, ideas and opportunities could come back. To keep the frequency open, place your board in a corner of your room, by your desk, next to your mirror, on the fridge, or somewhere else where you'll come across it a few times a day.

5. **LISTEN.** It's unlikely that the universe will respond immediately no matter say, loud and clear, "Okay—here you go!" After all, it gets a lot of messages. But I believe that if you listen closely, you *will* get a message back. It might be advice left in a voicemail, a book you happen to read at just the right moment, or something you notice a

friend doing. It might be a dream, a line in a song, or a conversation with a trusted adult. When that voice speaks, it's important to listen—no matter how you get the message, and whether you think it's coming from the universe or from within your own heart and mind. And while you wait for the voice, think about how you can *earn* what you desire. What can *you* do to make your dreams a reality?

6. **TAKE ACTION.** Your vision board is just that—a board full of great ideas—until you start taking action. When you explore your hopes and dreams, ideas will come. When you know what you're looking for, you'll be able to spot opportunities. So pay attention and be ready to respond with confidence, discipline, and bravado. Over time, you are creating a new reality. And a vision board is a great tool to help lift yourself into your desired future.

A FAIRY-TALE ENDING

Walt Disney, one of the great visionaries in animation history, summed it up well: "We keep moving forward—opening up new doors and doing new things—because we're curious. And curiosity keeps leading us down new paths."

If Harper Grace's dream board helped her go from rock bottom to Hollywood, I wonder where you can go and what you can do, no matter where you are right now. It begins with curiosity and continues with a dream. And it leads to recovery, self-discovery, and reinvention. Don't stay stuck in your past. It's time to get moving.

CHAPTER **2**

SHINE A FLASHLIGHT ON YOUR DREAMS IN THE DARK

I love dreams. They fascinate me.

This experience we have inside us, where our brain can take us just about anywhere, while our body lies still in bed. It's amazing.

For example, consider dreams that spark déjà vu. Have you ever had one of those? When you hear someone say or do something during the day, and it's like a switch goes off in your brain: *I dreamed of this exact moment last night!*

How about a dream with a commercial break? You are in the middle of a dream storyline, and you wake up, fall back asleep, and continue dreaming that same story until it ends.

Or visitation dreams? The perfectly clear and vivid experience of seeing a family member or friend who died but somehow returned to life when your eyes closed.

And what about the dreams with you and your celebrity or school crush? (I don't need the details.)

What intrigues *you* about dreams? We could probably talk about this all day, but right now I want to talk about how you can use your dreams to grow emotionally. First, let's make sure we're on the same page about the origin of dreams.

WHAT IS A DREAM?

A dream is a story that your brain creates while you sleep. It can happen during any stage of sleep, but most often occurs during REM (rapid eye movement) sleep, when parts of your brain become very active.

As Matthew Walker explains in his book *Why We Sleep*, a lot is going on in the mind during this stage. There's increased activity in several key areas of the brain:

- **Visuospatial region:** This area in the back of the brain activates your visual awareness so you can see a story in your mind's eye.
- **Motor cortex:** This is the part of the brain that plans and controls movement, like riding a bike.
- **Amygdala and cingulate cortex:** These are the deep emotion centers of the brain, where your feelings take control of the steering wheel—and the story. These domains are up to 30 percent more active during REM sleep than when you're awake!

- **The hippocampus and surrounding regions:** These areas support your autobiographical memory, helping you remember the story when you wake up.

While all these areas are activated, there's also *deactivation* of the prefrontal cortex, which is where your logic and reason come from.

To simplify and summarize: in the dream state, your brain records a video of a highly emotional story through some movement with characters, objects, and you. But at the same time, the storyline has little to no logic or reason. Then you wake up and your prefrontal cortex is reactivated, reviews the video, and thinks, *that was wild!*

SHINE THE FLASHLIGHT

Sigmund Freud and Carl Jung, two renowned psychologists in the area of dream study, had differing theories about the purpose of dreams.

Freud argued that our dreams are stories our brains create to hide our wishes, while Jung believed our dreams reveal our wishes. But recent research may suggest that what dreams really do is reveal our emotions.

Robert Stickgold, a sleep researcher and professor of psychiatry at Harvard Medical School, had 29 young adults keep journals of their waking days, along with their nighttime dreams, for two weeks. He found that between 35 and 55 percent of the emotional themes the participants described during their days became part of their dreams at night.

So, if you worry a lot throughout the day, you might have an anxious dream that night. Or if you're excited about the gifts you may get for your birthday or an upcoming holiday, you might dream about a party. In a sense, maybe Freud and Jung are both right. Maybe our dreams do hide our wishes—our emotional ones. And, to Jung's point, we can reveal those wishes quickly, by simply paying more attention to the emotional current within our dreams and less to the details of the storyline itself.

Karen Frazier, the author of *The Dream Interpretation Handbook*, refers to this practice as "shadow work," in which a dreamer uses the content of their dreams to shine a light on the darker corners of their subconscious mind.

This is using the dream as a form of emotional inspection. You can use what you remember from your dream to perform a deep dive into what you may be hiding or unwilling to face.

Here are a few examples from dreams my former students described. (The stories have been slightly altered for anonymity and to protect the students' privacy.)

> "I was in kindergarten, walking down my school hallway with ice cream. Then a random fifth grader came up riding a unicorn, stole my ice cream, and rode away. I chased her all over the school and couldn't catch her. Eventually, I turned a corner and found the ice cream completely melted on the ground. The weirdest part is that I don't even like ice cream in real life, so I shouldn't have cared in the first place."

Could this dream really just be what it seems—a story about a unicorn and some ice cream? Or could it be about fear? Fear of going into kindergarten and being away from the comfort of home and family? Fear of being in a new environment, at a big school with big kids who may not be friendly?

"A year ago, I constantly worried about studying Spanish since I needed to get better at it to visit Mexico and talk with my grandparents, who didn't speak English. One night, I dreamt that I was in the room at my grandparents' house where my mom, sister, and I would be sleeping when we visited. I remember being unable to read, write, or speak Spanish and having a panic attack. I woke up right after and began studying much harder that morning. This dream taught me to take action instead of just wasting time worrying."

Upon awakening, this dreamer channeled the worries she had in her dream to create a plan. Her interpretation of the dream and the action she took as a result are a quintessential example of turning on the flashlight to create change. The same goes for our final dreamer:

"In my dream, I was going skydiving for the first time and beyond excited. I entered the airplane with my parachute. We took off and began increasing in elevation. I glanced out the window, and all of a sudden, the desire to jump that had been building throughout my dream began to fade away. The pilot asked me if I was ready. Before I could answer, I felt an immense amount of wind pushing my hair into my face—and then I was falling back down to Earth. It was the most amazing experience at first. I tried to pull the rip cord to open the parachute, but nothing happened. I panicked as I plummeted. My head spun, and I felt sick as the wind was beating on me. Suddenly, the most important moments in my short life spun around me in the air. I realized at that moment just how important life is. I realized you only live once. Then, I woke up."

In each of these examples, students shone their flashlights on the emotions underlying their dreams. Doing so helped them extract what they needed to understand.

THE DEA DREAM JOURNAL TECHNIQUE

For dreams I wish to interpret, I keep a dream journal by my bed. Each morning I jot down what I can remember of the previous night's dreams. Some of the ones I write about really do seem to be entirely random and quirky and provide little meaning. But for dreams that lend themselves to interpretation, the method I use for recording them might be helpful if you want to delve deeper into your dreams.

There are three parts to record in your journal: **description**, **emotion**, and **action**, which help you be your dream detective. I call it the DEA—not the Drug Enforcement Administration, but more like a Dream Exploration Administration. Here's how to do it:

1. **DESCRIPTION:** Describe the story—the content of the dream. Be as specific as possible. What's the setting? Are you at home? At school? Somewhere else? Are you indoors or outdoors? Is it storming, snowing, or sunny? Who are the characters, and what are they doing? Animals, people, objects? What's the plot? Think of rising action, climax, and resolution. What's the dialogue? What's being said aloud?

2. **EMOTION:** Explain any emotional themes you can pull from this story. Is it related to hope, fear, excitement, or grief? Is it the feeling that you can't succeed, no matter how much effort you put in? Is it the feeling of excitement about trying something new? Are there other dreams you've had with different content but a similar theme?

3. **ACTION:** Record a short plan for what you will do with that emotion moving forward. This plan might take the form of a few sentences, some bulleted points, a sketch, or some other visual. Is there a mantra you can repeat to yourself? Is there an old friendship you need to repair? Should you show courage and speak up about an issue that is important to you?

You can keep your dream journal in a notebook like I do, or you could type it into a phone, tablet, or computer. Or, if you prefer speaking rather than writing, your dream journal could even be a voice memo on your phone.

PUTTING IT ALL TOGETHER

As you read this book, you'll find other information to help you harness your dreams and put your interpretations into action. Chapter 7, "Survive the Zombie Student Apocalypse," will help by giving you ways to improve your sleep and therefore reach the level of REM sleep necessary for vivid dreaming. Chapter 4, "Name Your Dragons," will help strengthen your action plans *after* identifying each emotion from your dreams. All of these tools work together.

SWITCHING ON THE LIGHT

Have you heard of the Russian scientist Dmitri Mendeleev?

In the 1800s, he was struggling to understand and classify chemical elements fully. He worked on it very hard, for a very long time. Then, so the story goes, he had a dream in which he visualized elements organizing themselves into rows and columns. This dream helped Mendeleev find the inspiration he needed to create the periodic table, which orders the elements by atomic weight, revealing patterns in how the elements relate to each other.

No one really knows if this story about Mendeleev is true. But we *do* know that dreams can give us important insights. Could it be that some of your dreams contain the same type of opportunity? Not to organize the chemical elements of the world around you, but to organize the emotional elements of the world inside you?

There's only one way to find out. Shine your flashlight.

CHAPTER 3

CHECK YOUR TECH

Is a knife good or evil?

Someone could use a knife to hurt someone, which would be terrible. But what about a doctor who is performing surgery? They would use a knife to save a patient's life.

You can probably see where this is going. A knife itself is neither good nor evil. It's just a tool—and its nature is dependent on the person who holds it in their hand.

The same goes for technology tools like devices (from cell phones to smart TVs), social media, and video games. None are good or bad in and of themselves. But the why, where, when, and how of tech use can positively *or* negatively impact your mood, well-being, relationships, and school success. How is it affecting you, here and now? The questions that follow will help you determine if you are using tech in a hurtful or helpful way. Think about them and be as honest with yourself about the answers as you can.

WHY ARE YOU USING TECHNOLOGY?

There are a lot of positives to technology use. For one, it makes communication with friends and family *so* much more convenient. You don't have to use a dial-up phone, write a letter and take it to a mailbox, or send messages via a carrier pigeon. Instead, you can simply press a few buttons on your phone, maybe throw in some playful emojis, and hit send. Within seconds, the message is delivered. The same goes on the receiving end. Whether through a text or FaceTime, tech can forge an instant connection.

Secondly, it has created a vibrant venue for self-expression. You can use Instagram to share a picture you've made with Procreate, head to TikTok to show off a dance move you've been working on, or use a funny Snapchat filter to provide laughter to yourself and your friends.

Thirdly, gaming can transport you to entirely new dimensions you could never visit in real life. With a VR headset, you can battle Darth Vader with lightsabers or play putt-putt golf in outer space.

There are other positives too, but you get the idea.

However, some people also use tech—or, more specifically, social media—for external validation. That means seeking approval or attention from outside yourself—from others. The problem is, that kind of approval is unreliable and out of your control.

One day, you might wake up looking like a supermodel, and on another day, not even close. One week, your muscles are bulging, and the next, not so much. You post selfies on your supermodel days, and the likes and comments roll in. "You're so pretty." "You're so handsome." Those compliments can give you a confidence boost, but they can have a cost too. Maybe you begin to feel like you have a reputation you've got to live up to, and that pressure becomes a burden. Or maybe the positive feedback creates a hunger for more. It can stoke a desire for continual affirmation through an external like button, rather than an internal love button. You're looking to the outside world for acceptance, rather than looking within. And when things change and those likes dry up—which they may, for reasons you can't always know, predict, or prevent—where will you go for approval?

Or say you posted a witty video that went viral. You were the talk of the town. "Yo, you were in that video . . . that was amazing!" "I saw your video and shared it with all my friends. So funny." You feel validated in that spotlight moment, but after a few weeks, the praise dies down. People's attention moves on to the next thing. *I've got to make another hit video*, you think. That's how social media can go from positive to negative and hook you in an unhealthy way. Like a drug, it can create a short-term euphoria that keeps you coming back for more.

Okay, though—let's consider another possibility. What if you feel like you can present and maintain a "perfect" image online all the time? Even then, it still isn't realistic to think you'll receive constant compliments. On any given day, other people might be busy, or envious, or just in a bad mood. All kinds of things can keep them from hitting "like" or saying something nice. Nevertheless, some people have trouble resisting the pull of that approval. It's understandable. Compliments usually feel good. So it's also understandable if sometimes you feel the need to be tied to your phone and constantly posting, in search of the next "likes and shares" boost. At the same time, if you've started to depend on that boost, how crummy does it feel when you *don't* get it?

I know it's easy for me to say you don't need other people to tell you you're beautiful or strong. That you don't need a digital trophy, a thousand likes, or to make a viral video. That you don't need praise to feel pretty or powerful. Easy to say, but sometimes not so easy to live by.

Fortunately, there's a solution. It doesn't happen overnight, but it's powerful. When you possess *internal* validation—unconditional self-confidence—you don't need to rely on approval from others. Sounds great, right? But *how* can you achieve this self-confidence?

First, it's essential to identify your values and your purposes (you can have several) for existence. What do you truly care about? Loving-kindness, presence, justice, family, academic success, swimming, or the theater? And, on a deeper level, what purpose do you feel called to? How can you craft meaning by exercising your values? Rescuing, caring for, or adopting animals in your community? Carrying on family traditions? Working toward a law degree or reforming the legal system? Helping people smile and laugh by performing on stage? (Oh, and by the way: If these questions feel really, really big and hard to answer, check out chapter 8 for more information.)

Once your values and purposes are clear, it's time for the next level: acting in accordance with them. Are you living true to your nature?

If living in the present moment and being connected to family are meaningful in your mind, but you spend most of your Thanksgiving scrolling through your phone instead of catching up with your grand-mother, something's off. But if you put your phone in your pocket for 30 minutes and ask her how she's doing, what she's been into lately, and what life was like when she was a teen, you are crafting connection and meaning. When our values and our choices are in harmony, it's a beautiful symphony. When they aren't, it's an off-key song that hurts the ears and the heart.

Tech can become a distraction from working on your self-confidence. This isn't surprising—after all, it's a lot easier to spend time online than it is to put in the work of exercising your values and stepping toward your purpose. Nevertheless, it's ultimately less fulfilling. By contrast, building your self-confidence takes time and effort, but it's well worth it. It helps you approach your tech use and social media with a full tank of self-worth, rather than waiting to have it filled up. You are living a life of authenticity, so what you post online becomes a manifestation and extension of that self, rather than a façade you've built in hopes of impressing people. And when you feel confident sharing your truths and your stories without worrying what others will think, that confidence allows you to joyfully entertain, encourage, comfort, inspire, and connect with friends, family, and fans—online and off. Internal validation, not external validation—living a life congruent with your values and your self-worth. *That's* beautiful. The Greek philosopher Epictetus said it best: "If your choices are beautiful, so too will you be."

WHERE ARE YOU USING TECHNOLOGY?

In the podcast *How to Build a Happy Life,* happiness researcher Arthur Brooks points out that you can have friends and still be lonely.

Technology can add to this loneliness. For example, have you ever had this experience? You're at a concert or some other event with your friends, but all of you spend the whole time taking pictures or videos and checking your phones for messages and replies. When that happens, you aren't fully experiencing the show with each other. You're experiencing it with your phones. You aren't really living in the moment. Instead, you're documenting a future memory.

But friendships are built on shared experiences. Eye contact. Talking and listening. Singing together. Dancing together. Authentic connections. That is what turns *me* into *us*.

So watch for times when you're together with others, but not truly connected. Ask yourself if this is a moment where technology is putting up a barrier between you and the people around you. If the answer is yes, try turning off the tech or putting it away.

WHEN ARE YOU USING TECHNOLOGY?

If you wake up and immediately reach for your phone to begin scrolling through social media, emails, or texts, you are giving some of your power away first thing in the morning. There's no telling what you'll see—from political vitriol online, to critical feedback from your teacher in an email, to bullying in a text thread.

On the other hand, if you get out of bed and start your day by setting goals for the day, checking your calendar, listening to an upbeat podcast, meditating, or playing energetic music, you're starting your day off right. It might take time to find the morning routine that works for you, but try starting each morning with positive intention and activities that boost your power and energy rather than potentially sapping it. Then, once you're heading into the day on a good note, you can begin digging into reading your emails, texts, and other tech tasks that could be positive *or* negative.

Similarly, using tech right before bed can have drawbacks too. Looking at a screen can disrupt your sleep cycle, for instance. You'll find more about this in chapter 7, but the basic idea is that your devices emit blue light, which sends a signal to your brain to focus and pay attention. The brain doesn't need that message when it's time to go to sleep. Instead, it requires the "Do Not Disturb" chill mode. But you can still use your tech to help you wind down your day without staring at a screen and getting a big dose of blue light. Turn on a sleep story podcast or a sleep meditation from an app like Calm, or start a playlist of soothing music. Then set the device aside—face-down, ideally, or with the screen covered—and focus on the sound. If you like to read right before bed, you could read a book in print, or read an ebook (as long as it's on an e-reader that doesn't emit blue rays).

HOW ARE YOU USING TECHNOLOGY?

We all know that tech and the vast online world have a lot of information and wisdom to offer. But there are plenty of distractions too. So one thing to consider when it comes to how you use tech is whether you could be taking greater advantage of it as a portal to wisdom and growth.

Think about the ancient story of Mimir and Odin, which Neil Gaiman retells in his book *Norse Mythology*. Mimir lived in Jotunheim, the home of the giants. Every day, he drank from his well, the well of wisdom. One day, Odin left his hometown and traveled a dangerous journey to Jotunheim. When he finally got there, he asked Mimir for one drink from his well. But Mimir said no. Only he was allowed to drink from the well of wisdom.

Odin continued to plead with him for one drink. At last, Mimir said he would only give him a drink for a price. "Your eye is my price," he told Odin.

Odin's response? "Give me a knife."

He removed his eye, gave it to Mimir, and drank from the well. Wisdom flowed through his entire body. For the rest of his life, he saw the world more clearly with one eye than he ever did with two.

Okay, don't panic. You don't have to sacrifice your eye to Mimir to gain wisdom. But you *may* want to trade in some types of tech use for others. For example, if video games or social media scrolling tend to be distractions for you, you could offer up some of that time to make room for other online pursuits that offer greater rewards. Sites like edX (edx.org) and Coursera (coursera.org) offer a huge range of classes for free from universities all over the world. Many educational and informational podcasts are also available at no cost. And at sites like Project Gutenberg (gutenberg.org), you can read thousands of ebooks for free.

For a fee, you can also take courses through Wondrium (wondrium.com) or MasterClass (masterclass.com), which offers videos from instructors like Gordon Ramsay (cooking), Jane Goodall (conservation), Judy Blume (writing), Christina Aguilera (singing), Amanda Gorman (poetry), and Steph Curry (basketball). Or you can subscribe to major news sources and read articles, watch videos, and more.

When you master the art of using technology as a portal to wisdom, you will be able to see the world more clearly than ever before.

WHAT ARE YOU DOING *WITHOUT* TECHNOLOGY?

It's true that hitting a fitness goal on a smartwatch, seeing you've gotten a lot of likes on an Instagram photo, or receiving exciting news in an email can give you a surge of endorphins and dopamine (happiness-stimulating hormones released in your brain). Fortunately, there are plenty of screen-free activities that do the same! Here are a few ideas:

- Instead of playing video games, play board games or card games.
- Instead of using social media, socialize with friends at a mall, a coffee shop, a party, or someone's home.

- Instead of watching a TV show or movie with animal characters, take your own pet for a walk or play with them.
- Instead of spending time on your phone at family gatherings, be with the people who are there. Ask older family members about their childhoods, stories, and life lessons they could share.
- Instead of viewing an animated show, create your own images in a notebook. Draw a cast of characters, whether they're fictional, historical, or from your life.
- Instead of talking on FaceTime or Zoom, have lunch with a friend or family member and talk face-to-face.
- Instead of checking your step count on a fitness tracker or smartwatch, play a pick-up basketball or soccer game where you know you're getting exercise without having to check the data constantly.
- Instead of listening to music through your headphones, create your own tunes by singing or playing an instrument.
- Instead of watching a fictional storyline play out on a TV show you're streaming, sit outside and read a fascinating story.
- Instead of taking pictures with your phone of yourself and your friends, go on a nature walk and take in the whole panorama around you. Try to mentally save the beautiful scenes you take in.

WHAT WILL YOU HOLD CLOSEST?

Now that you've answered all these questions, do you have a better perspective on your use of your phone and other devices? Has a clearer picture formed of how tech can affect your mood and your life—for better or worse? Do you have ideas for what you might like to try and change?

As Adam Alter points out in a class from Calm (calm.com) called "Social Media and Screen Addiction," a theory in psychology called *propinquity* says that the things that are closest to you in physical space have the biggest impact on your psychological experience of the world. And what's closest to many of us, most of the time? Our phones.

Don't get me wrong—there's nothing inherently wrong with technology, and there's nothing wrong with keeping your phone close to you. Remember, a phone is just a tool. What matters is how you use it. So tune into your feelings and your experiences, and make an intentional effort to not be *so* tied to the digital world that your phone is literally and figuratively the closest thing to you at all times. Instead, make it one part of your environment and your life, along with books, board games, friends, family, nature, exercise, restaurants, shops, music, art—whatever you want to hold close to your heart.

CHAPTER **4**

NAME YOUR DRAGONS

There was once a dragon who guarded a cave full of ancient treasures.

Many warriors tried to defeat him to get to the treasures. They used swords, shields, and flaming arrows, but nothing worked.

Then one day, a calm warrior walked up to the dragon and whispered something in its ear. After a moment, the dragon stepped to the side and let the warrior enter. This warrior soon returned with a bag full of treasures.

When the other warriors asked him his secret, he responded, " You cannot defeat the dragon in battle, but it will let you pass if you call it by its name."

The same goes for the emotional dragons we all have inside our minds. We can fight them all we want, but we will only be able to move through them and past them if we can identify them. You transform into a calm warrior when you stop battling and acknowledge how you feel. So who are these dragons, specifically?

THE SEVEN DRAGONS

According to Paul Ekman, a psychologist who specializes in the study of emotions, all people experience seven primary emotions:

- Sadness
- Surprise
- Fear
- Anger
- Disgust
- Contempt
- Happiness

While Ekman uses colors to distinguish and discuss these emotions, I say we go even bolder and think of them as dragons. In the chart on the next page, you'll find a name I've given to each emotional dragon, and an example of how each one might show up in your life.

To identify a feeling is to name your dragon. That is *emotional intelligence*. But imagine that even after you whisper the dragon's name, it continues to block your path. Maybe it isn't breathing fire in your direction, but you're still not ready to charge past it. How do you get through?

Part of your hero's journey is to learn how identify, accept, and work through these powerful emotions. This chapter will help you not only identify and name each dragon, but also learn how to calm each one—both in the moment, and later, when a feeling may resurface. Let's say you make it past the first dragon. As you continue on your way, you encounter many more dragons. Some of them may let you pass into the cave, but others may put obstacles in your path. What if one attacks? What if another tries to snatch you up with its claws? That's when it's essential not just to know their names, but also to how to soothe them with a potion made specifically for them. Better to name *and* tame them. Taming your emotional dragons is *emotional regulation*.

Here are the dragons:

NIGHTFIRE: THE SADNESS DRAGON	**Sadness may be sparked by losing someone or something important to you.** *"My boyfriend broke up with me and I really miss him."*
THUNDERHEED: THE SURPRISE DRAGON	**Surprise can come when we experience something unexpected.** *"I can't believe I got a C on that test. I did the study guide, went to tutoring, and felt like I aced it."*
HOPESLAYER: THE FEAR DRAGON	**We feel fear in the face of a threat, whether it's real or imaginary.** *"I know he's going to try to fight me next time he sees me in the hallway."*
FIREBREATHER: THE ANGER DRAGON	**Anger often flares when we're being treated unfairly by someone or when we're prevented from having something we want.** *"I'm so mad I didn't get the part. I practiced hard for weeks and nailed my audition."*
ABHORRLOTH: THE DISGUSTED DRAGON	**You can think of disgust as the yuck factor. We feel disgusted when something we taste, smell, hear touch, or see grosses us out.** *"Ugh, I just wanted a snack and I ended up biting into a rotten apple."*
BLOODEYE: THE CONTEMPT DRAGON	**Contempt is a strong dislike for a person or group because of their perceived or actual actions, possibly viewing them as inferior in some way.** *"That guy always says the dumbest things. I wish our teacher would stop making me be his partner in class."*
JOYTEMIS: THE HAPPINESS DRAGON	**Happiness comes from pleasure inspired by any of the five senses, or by a sense of connection with others.** *"My team just won the championship! Yesssss! This is the best feeling ever!"*

THE SEVEN POTIONS

The potions to soothe these dragons come from some of the wisest philosophers in history, the Stoics. These ancient Greeks and Romans knew how to calm their emotions through logical thinking. The specific ingredients of these potions have been passed down to us through the words of some of the most famous Stoics—Seneca, a skilled politician and writer; Epictetus, a teacher and an enslaved person; and Marcus Aurelius, the last great emperor of Rome. We can use these classical teachings and apply them in modern times.

Read on to find out how.

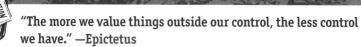

SADNESS: DICHOTOMY OF CONTROL

"The more we value things outside our control, the less control we have." —Epictetus

Ryan Holiday, a leading author on Stoic principles, talks about a strategy that can help with stress and sadness. If you're sad about a situation, open a journal and draw a line down the middle. Title the left column "Not Up to Me," and the right column "Up to Me." On the left, list things you don't have 100 percent control over, such as "My boyfriend broke up with me." In the right column, list things you *do* have 100 percent control over, like, "I can talk to no one about this, or I can share my feelings with a close friend." When you are finished writing, tear off the left side of the paper and throw it away. Keep the right side and act based on your written reflections and sphere of influence.

SURPRISE: AMOR FATI

"Don't seek for everything to happen as you wish it would, but rather wish that everything happens as it actually will—then your life will flow well." —Epictetus

Amor fati means "lover of fate." The idea here is that whatever happens—no matter how unexpected or surprising—we can choose to embrace it as destiny. And we can find *something* to love about it and work with that. This doesn't mean you have to love the rotten part of the apple. But you *can* embrace the positive experience of having food at all, even if it isn't perfect. You can use the experience to remember all the delicious, ripe apples you've eaten. Is it possible you took some of them for granted? If so, amor fati helps you see that. It says, *I'm glad I bit into this rotten apple, because I needed a reminder to be grateful for fresh food when I do eat it. Next time I eat a crisp apple, I'll take the time to really savor its taste and texture.* (If this idea interests you, you'll find more about amor fati in chapter 15: "End with Gratitude.")

FEAR: PREMEDITATIO MALORUM

"The unexpected blows of fortune fall heaviest and most painfully, which is why the wise man thinks about them in advance." —Seneca

Premeditatio malorum is the idea of negative visualization, or anticipating the things that can go wrong. It can be troubling if you do it all the time or if it causes nothing but worry. But it can work in your favor if you lead with logic over emotion. For example, let's say some guy told you he would jump you in the hallway. Have you told a trusted adult (for example, a parent, teacher, principal, or other adult)? Is there a classmate you can walk with who can help you feel safer? Could you take a different route to your next class? In the longer term, in case this happens again, could you take self-defense classes so you feel more confident protecting yourself?

When you use this potion wisely, it can help you think through a situation and prepare for how you will respond if something you're afraid of does happen. In turn, that can keep you from freezing with fear.

ANGER: FUEL FOR THE FIRE

"A blazing fire makes flame and brightness out of everything that is thrown into it." —Marcus Aurelius

Let's say you have a strong passion for acting and invest a lot of time and energy into getting a role you want. You study your lines each night and make sure you know every word. But despite your efforts, you don't get the part. You might be angry because you didn't receive what you felt you earned. You may also feel like a failure or embarrassed because you didn't get the part. You want to yell at the director and the actor who got your part—and maybe anyone else who happens to be around.

Anger is a very powerful emotion, and it can be hard to control. But lashing out rarely fixes anything, and it can make everything worse. A better course of action is to use your anger as fuel. In the audition example, you could use it to strengthen your acting acumen. Rather than shrinking back into the darkness, begin preparing for the next play's tryouts. And don't just stick to your normal practice. Try some new techniques. Talk to and observe the people who landed roles. See if you can sign up for acting classes online or in person. Watch videos of performers you admire. Have a courageous conversation with the director about what you need to do to improve. Don't go dark with your anger. Let it make your light shine even brighter.

DISGUST: SELF-DISCIPLINED SELF-TALK

"Be tolerant with others and strict with yourself." —Marcus Aurelius

Here's a scenario: Your friend invited you over for dinner at their home with their family. While serving the meal, they accidentally gave you a piece of food that was rotten or undercooked. It's likely that you'll have an immediate reaction of being grossed out. That's natural. But in that moment, it can also be important for you to practice self-discipline and not make a scene. You can remind yourself that your friend cares about you and that their intention wasn't to cause disgust. Instead, they just made a mistake—one that might embarrass them. In response, you can practice grace by quietly and discreetly letting them know what happened, or by avoiding the topic altogether. Focus on their intention instead of the result. Respond in a way you hope your friend would if the roles were reversed.

CONTEMPT: SYMPATHEIA

"Look after each other. Life is short—the fruit of this life is a good character and acts for the common good." —Marcus Aurelius

Imagine your teacher partners you up again for another class project with a student you can't stand. They don't have a full grasp of the course material and, in your opinion, their ideas aren't very creative. You feel like a lot of the academic workload falls to you, and it seems that you must play two roles at once—student in the class, and teacher to this other student.

Sympatheia is the Stoic idea of an interconnectedness among all things in the universe. In this scenario, it can include a connection between this student and you—even if you don't think that's possible.

How to activate sympatheia? First, ruminate on reasons why your fellow student might be struggling. Maybe they feel really lonely or lost or even stupid. Maybe they're distracted by hunger because they don't always have breakfast. Maybe they have an invisible disability. And maybe that's why you keep getting paired up with them—because the teacher of this class knows you have the skills *and* the compassion to be a good partner to someone who could use a little extra support.

Secondly, embrace them and be grateful for them. In some way, shape, or form, this person is meant to connect with you. And interconnectedness always offers a chance to grow. It might be an opportunity to practice patience, openness, humility, or servant-leadership. And it could give you the chance to be a part of something bigger and outside of yourself.

HAPPINESS: MEMENTO MORI

"True happiness is to enjoy the present without anxious dependence on the future." —Seneca

You just won the trophy! Congratulations! This is your moment, and you should enjoy it—*in* the moment.

And . . . then what? Just as dwelling on past mistakes doesn't always serve us well, it's also wise not to try and force your present happiness into the future. Enjoy the here and now, rather than immediately saying, "We're going to win it again next year!" Instead of clutching that trophy in a death grip, hold it gently. The truth is, happiness comes and goes. It won't last forever. In Stoic philosophy, this is called memento mori. Remember that you will die. Remember that all things pass. Remember that all seasons end. Remember that you may never have another moment like this again, so savor it as fully as you can.

This fleeting nature is one reason happiness might need "taming" at times. But there are other reasons too. For instance, when you win that trophy, your happiness could cause you to *over*-celebrate, or to rub your victory in an opponent's face. To tame happiness in that moment would be to show humility, briefly celebrate with your teammates and coach, and be considerate enough to meet the other team at midfield or half court, give them a high five, a handshake, or a hug, and tell them, "Great game."

Or, what if happiness is causing harm to yourself or to someone else? Some people who use drugs or alcohol say they do so because it's the only thing that makes them happy. But that's a destructive kind of happiness.

Lastly, it's important to tame happiness because of what Buddhists call impermanence. This is a lot like memento mori. It means that no one is happy forever. So if you start chasing the feeling and obsessing over it— when your reaction to happiness moves from "I enjoy this" to "I need to feel this all the time"—that's an unhealthy state of mind. It can lead you to prioritize happiness over purpose, and sets you up for disappointment. When I think about this idea, I always feel like Thomas Jefferson *almost* got it right: Rather than "life, liberty, and the pursuit of happiness," I suggest we strive for "life, liberty, and the pursuit of purpose."

Some of these dragon-taming techniques may seem daunting at first. I get that. But it might help to know that the only real alternative is emotional suppression. Emotional suppression is when you bury or deflect your feelings and refuse to engage with them. Emotional suppression can lead to lower cognition (less clear thinking), reduced memory, and in some cases, even depression.

Lastly, please remember to give yourself grace. As neurologist Frances E. Jensen and journalist Amy Ellis Nutt point out in their book *The Teenage Brain,* adolescence is a time when your hormones are incredibly active. Some of these hormones are released into parts of the brain called your limbic system. And your limbic system also plays a key role in your emotions. This is part of why many people seek out high-emotion experiences during their teen years. For example, some like to pursue thrill-seeking adventures such as ziplining. Others may want emotionally charged experiences from watching shows about dark, sad themes—or dancing wildly to hype music.

So if this is an era of emotion in your life, try not to be hard on yourself when you become exhausted trying to slay the dragon. Instead, step back, give yourself a moment, and then advance with the wisdom of the Stoic philosophers.

CHAPTER 5

STARE INTO THE SNAKE

Learning to deal with emotions in healthy ways may be one of the most underrated strategies for finding your purpose and blazing your own trail. I think that's partly because it takes so much commitment, so some people shy away from it. But it could be one of the most important things you do.

A huge component of emotional well-being is *presence*. It's about being fully engaged with what you're experiencing—whether it's sadness, joy, fear, excitement, loneliness, anticipation, or worry. It's about not trying to escape your feelings, but about being daring enough to sit with them and work through them in the moment.

Think about this story: There was once a girl who was constantly afraid. She was scared she would fail math and would not make the sports team. She worried that she'd lose all her friends and that her parents would get divorced. Finally, she talked to a teacher she trusted. She told him that she wanted to get rid of all her fears. He suggested meditation and something called the Square Breath.

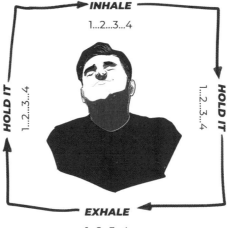

So one night she went to a tent and lit three candles. Then she sat on her mat, closed her eyes, and focused her attention on her breath. But after a few minutes, nothing had changed. She was still afraid.

A few seconds later, she heard a rustling in the tent. She opened her eyes to see a venomous viper on the other side of the candles, swaying back and forth, staring straight at her. The girl froze.

Throughout the night, their eyes remained locked as she practiced her square breath: four seconds of breathing in through the nose, a four-second hold, four seconds of breathing out through the mouth, and another four-second hold. She was beginning to feel calm.

But then her anxiety shot up again as one of the candles burned out. Then another. She caught one last view of the snake as the final candle ran out of wax, and the tent went completely dark. The girl began to tremble, and tears filled her eyes. She felt a fear so heavy that she collapsed and cried herself to sleep.

In the morning, she awoke. She looked around the tent. No snake. She looked at her body. No bites. She got up, walked out, and felt the sun on her face. For the first time in a long time, she was fearless.

Buddhist teacher and author Pema Chödrön said it well: "To be fearless isn't really to overcome fear, it's to come to know its nature."

What is the value in knowing the nature of fear? So often, when we come face-to-face with fear, it makes us want to turn and run away as fast as we can. But the problem with this is that we aren't just running from what scares us. We're also running from our potential.

Suppose you fear that you'll fail math, so you simply give up. Maybe you could have gone to tutoring during your free period and at least pulled a C, but instead you earn an F. Or you might be so afraid you won't make the volleyball team that you don't even bother trying out. But what if, because of that, you don't meet another player at tryouts who would've asked you to join a team at the rec center?

Fear takes you out of the sport of life. It's a self-fulfilling prophecy in the worst way. You become a spectator instead of a gladiator. And you never know what you'll miss when fear keeps you sidelined.

On the other hand, when you develop the inner strength to sit with your fear—to stay in the tent and stare into the snake—you also develop the skills to move through that fear and not let it control, limit, or diminish you. And, in a larger sense, it's important to learn to sit with *all* your emotions and work through them rather than pushing them down or running away from them. Because one way or another, they'll catch up with you eventually. Some research suggests that suppressing a feeling can actually create physical stress in your body. By contrast, when you can experience and communicate the full range of your emotions in a healthy way, you'll have more authentic relationships with others, a better understanding of yourself, and greater well-being overall.

Here are some techniques that can be useful as you work on confronting fear and other emotions:

- **Walking and talking with a trusted friend or family member.** It's possible they may have had similar emotions and experiences and could offer you some advice. It's comforting to know you are not the only who's been through a tough situation—and it also helps other people better understand why you are feeling the way you are.

- **Journaling.** Write about the feeling and make a list of possible ways you could respond, both negatively and positively. Put a line through the ones that are unhealthy responses, and circle the healthy ones. Commit to doing one of the latter.

- **Meditating with calm music.** When your emotions start to feel too big and too strong, and you're tempted to ignore or repress them, try listening to some slow, soothing tunes without lyrics and breathing deeply. This can support you in slowing down racing thoughts and clearing brain fog.

- **Counseling.** If you're struggling to deal with your emotions and feel like you can't handle them on your own, talk to a parent about the possibility of seeing a counselor. A skilled counselor can help you find the right words to express externally what you are feeling internally. They might also teach you about brain-based techniques such as cognitive behavioral therapy.

- **Taking a physical approach.** Exercise can help you release the tension that can be caused by strong emotions. If you or your family can afford it, you might also talk to a parent about trying massage therapy, which can help reduce the physical stress on your body and, in turn, help you access and work through your feelings. You could also look for videos on YouTube showing how to do yoga, tai chi, and other stress-busting exercises, or simply go on a brisk walk or light jog for 15 to 30 minutes.

- **Planning a reward for yourself.** After I speak in front of a large audience—which means confronting my trepidation of public speaking—I treat myself to a donut. (A chocolate-covered donut with sprinkles, to be precise.) I know my treat might sound silly, but it works for me! Try coming up with some small, creative reward that you can look forward to after doing something outside of your comfort zone—or, as I like to think about it, something inside of your challenge zone.

Emotional awareness—whether around fear, worry, or any other feeling—is not a passive state. It's active, living with an open heart. It's about knowing what to do with each emotion—not hiding from it, not running from it, but having the courage to see it, stay with it, and own it, rather than giving it the power to own you.

CHAPTER 6

GROUND YOURSELF

Ground yourself.

I'm not saying lock yourself up in a room and sit in the corner. I mean literally *ground* yourself. Go outside, and, if you live in a place where the weather permits, take off your shoes and socks. Sit in a chair, on a stoop, or on the ground, and place your bare feet in grass, sand, or dirt for 30 minutes a day.

This practice—called *earthing* or *grounding*—is a form of nature therapy. According to Clinton Ober, Stephen Sinatra, and Martin Zucker, it can reduce inflammation in your body, eliminate chronic pain, improve blood flow, reduce stress, increase energy, and improve sleep. Their book about this, *Earthing*, is intriguing and well-researched.

But why would this work? The essential theory goes that, when two conductive objects make contact, electrons will flow from where they are abundant to where they are not. Earth's surface has a negative electrical charge, meaning that it's filled with electrons that aren't attached to molecules. These electrons are also called free electrons, and they're attracted to objects with a positive electrical charge—like, for instance, the human body. However, the book's authors theorize that you need direct contact for this transfer to happen, and the soles of your shoes can cut off the connection. Plus, the authors write that the foot's sole is packed with 1,300 nerve endings per square inch. Why might so many nerve endings be concentrated in that location of the body? Perhaps to keep us in touch with the earth.

Try spending 30 minutes a day with your bare feet on the ground or in the grass. I put this into practice whenever I can, which could be while I'm doing chores outside, reading on my back porch, or sometimes even while taking a walk. It took a while to get used to being barefoot while walking, but now I love it. As you do this, you might read a book, play a board game, eat a snack, or stare at the clouds. Or even check your social media, watch YouTube, or do your homework. Just do it *grounded*.

(If you live in a colder climate where this isn't possible or comfortable for much of the year, try to take advantage of those days when the temperature *is* right. Or, if you get the chance to visit a warmer climate, seize the opportunity to ground yourself there.)

I can see you rolling your eyes while reading this. *Is this guy a hippie? Is he weird?* Yes. I am weird. Weird about my mental health. Weird about my physical health. Weird enough to try techniques that might help me on my journey, even when they sound strange.

Do you want the same results as everyone else? Then do what the majority is doing. Follow the norm and keep your shoes on.

Or, do you want to be a true trailblazer? Then try something like this, something out-of-the-box and unconventional—even if you feel unsure or skeptical at first. Embrace your exile from the typical. It doesn't have to be lonely. It can be a peaceful path leading from a present of exploration to a future of discovery.

If you feel comfortable, try playing baseball, soccer, or frisbee without shoes once in a while. Or, if you are into gardening and doing yard work, take your socks and shoes off to do so (as long as it's safe). If you go walking through fields or woods and find a stretch of smooth and safe terrain, take your shoes off for a little while. (You could even take a towel and a spray bottle with water to rinse your feet before you head home.) If you like fishing, try doing it barefoot. Or simply sit outside with your phone, a tablet, or a book—and your feet planted firmly on the ground. There are so many options!

THE BETTER YOU BREATHE, THE BETTER YOU LIVE

Another way to ground yourself is through your breath. In many combat sports like boxing, jujutsu, and mixed martial arts, the concept of mental and physical grounding is ever-present. Grounded techniques and movements can help you keep your balance and protect yourself from attack by your opponent. But in boxing and in life, calculated, grounded movements combined with rhythmic breathing can help you go the distance.

One of the most calming breathing exercises out there is called the 4-7-8 breath. It's simple to do: Breathe in through your nose for four seconds, hold for seven seconds, and breathe out through your nose for eight seconds. If you repeat this for two to three minutes, it can bring you back to the present, reduce cortisol (a stress hormone in your brain), and even minimize some effects of anxiety.

Another breathing exercise is to put one hand down on a desk, a table, or your lap with your fingers spread wide. With the index finger from your other hand, trace up and around each finger, beginning with the thumb and ending with the pinky finger. As you move up each finger, inhale through your nose. As you move down the other side of each finger, exhale through your nose.

This could work before a big test, after a family argument, before performing at a concert, or during a panic attack. As Jay Shetty points out in his book *Think Like a Monk,* "The only thing that stays with you from the moment you are born until the moment you die is your breath." The better you breathe, the more alive you are.

CHAPTER 7

SURVIVE THE ZOMBIE STUDENT APOCALYPSE

There are Zombie Students in your school building, and they are increasing in number. Have you seen one?

I saw one at our school just last week. I swear his flesh looked green and withered. Saliva was dripping from his mouth in slo-mo. The bags under his eyes made him look older than me! He barely breathed as he stumbled down the hallway with his bookbag and Dr. Pepper. It was like each step was pulling him closer to the grave.

Alarmed, I ducked into the nearest classroom and closed the door just before he passed by. I peeked through the window and shook my head in disbelief. *He was a straight-A student and the first-chair trombone player in band. I can't believe he's a zombie now.*

Okay, okay. Maybe this story is a *little* exaggerated. But the sad truth behind it is all too real: I've seen plenty of students turn into Zombie Students—not because of a bite, but because of sleep. Or rather, the lack of it.

After chugging a soft drink in their homeroom, they zone out and put their foreheads on their desks during the first block of their schedules. They close their eyes briefly, hoping to get back what they gave up when they became part of the apocalypse: a good night's rest.

But, for them, there was too much last-minute homework to complete, too many messages to check, too many videos to scroll through, and too many episodes to binge.

And for these future zombies, there *wasn't* a proactive plan for completing the work in the early evening. They didn't set boundaries for using screens before bed. So they stayed up late. After all, it's just a few fewer hours of sleep. There's not much difference between going to bed at 10 p.m. and 1 a.m., right? Wrong.

According to the American Academy of Sleep Medicine, you need eight to ten hours of sleep per night. When you forego sleep for something more enticing, your body doesn't forget—and you take the L every time. You:

- are low on energy the next day—not just for a few hours, but for the entire day
- may end up drinking caffeinated beverages, which briefly raise your energy level but cause you to crash when they wear off

- are grumpier, less patient, and more negative around your friends, classmates, teachers, and family
- weaken your immune system while learning in a classroom jammed full of germs
- upset the cycle of sleep your body expects for nights that follow

According to one research study cited in Tom Rath's book *Eat Move Sleep*, four hours of sleep loss can cognitively impair a person as much as a six-pack of beer. Would you show up to school drunk? I hope not. That would wreak havoc on your performance, not just academically but also in your sports or theatre performances, relationships, and emotional well-being.

Are you a Zombie Student already? Or could you be on your way to becoming one? Take this quiz to find out.

Zombie Student Quiz	*yes*	*no*
Are you unable to fall asleep after lying in bed for more than 15 minutes?		
Do you feel groggy in the mornings, even after you've gotten going and left home?		
Are you known for losing everyday objects like your phone, your papers, and your keys?		
Do you find yourself frequently yawning throughout the day?		

Zombie Student Quiz *cont.*	*yes*	*no*
Have you recently gone off on a family member or friend and immediately realized that you overreacted?		
Do you fall asleep in places other than your bed—like at school, on the bus, in the car, or at movie theaters?		
Does your stress level rise when you think about sleep?		
Do you ruminate and replay the same thoughts in your mind while you lie in bed?		

If you answered yes to four or more of these questions, you could qualify as a Zombie Student suffering from sleep deprivation or insomnia.

If that's the case, don't despair—your future isn't hopeless. Zombies are zombies forever, but Zombie Students can become healthy, well-rested teens again.

And, in a larger sense, if your desire is to blaze your own trail not just now but throughout your life, it's important to build a healthy sleep regimen *now*, or you may end up in trouble later on. Consider this: If you've ever played an open-world adventure game like *The Legend of Zelda: Breath of the Wild*, *Sneaky Sasquatch*, or *The Oregon Trail*, you know that sleep is built into the game. That's because these games take you on a long journey, and the body needs rest just as much as food, shelter, and equipment to survive the expedition.

The same is true in real life. A healthy sleep pattern at night provides sustainability through your future days—whether that means working at a job, raising kids, pursuing a hobby, exercising, spending quality time with friends, performing chores around the house, or traveling. Just about everything you do in life takes cognition, energy, and presence. That's why it's so key to do everything in your power to prevent sleep deprivation.

The best way to accomplish that goal? Ideally, aim for sleep that is *longer* and *better*, which means more time in bed with fewer interruptions until your alarm goes off. You can achieve longer and more efficient sleep by working on three factors: your Environment, Exercise, and Eating Habits. Let's call them the 3 Es for more Zs.

ENVIRONMENT

According to Shawn Stevenson in *Sleep Smarter*, our bodies are still wired like those of our ancient ancestors. During the day, they would be in sunlight on the move, hunting for animals and collecting food in the woods. When it got dark at night, they would rest and fall asleep. This created a particular circadian rhythm for the human body based on light and darkness, and that millennia-old rhythm still affects our bodies today.

So, the first question is, how much natural sunlight are you getting throughout the day? If you are stuck inside a lot, how can you expose your eyes and skin to the sun in small chunks? When you're at home, this could mean trying to get outside every hour or so during daylight, whether for a walk, a bike ride, or even just some time standing or sitting outdoors. Or, rather than aiming for a specific timeframe, you could use built-in natural breaks, like the end of a TV show episode you're watching or the end of a chapter you're reading. Consider it a noncommercial interruption and head outdoors for a few minutes.

In classrooms where you can pick your seat, choose one close to a window if there is one in the room. The same goes for the cafeteria, car, and school bus. When riding to or from school, try sitting in a window seat, not in the middle. Even on cloudy days and through glass, the more sun exposure, the better.

Nighttime is a whole different story. You want as little artificial light as possible. Our most significant obstacle to this is . . . you guessed it, our devices. Most televisions, tablets, and cell phones emit blue light, the same spectrum of light the sun sends out. It signals the brain to be alert and wake up—not exactly what you're aiming for right before bed. To combat this, you can try turning your devices into "Dark Mode" or "Night Mode" through the settings feature, which may turn off the blue light at sunset.

But setting your devices aside entirely is even more effective. So if you want to level up your sleep, the best strategy is to make a trade-in once it's time for bed: your phone for a book. One study, discussed in the TV series *Headspace Guide to Sleep,* compared teens who used iPads before sleeping to those who read a printed book before bed. The ones who used technology woke up more frequently throughout the night, while those who looked at a book had fewer interruptions to their sleep and were better rested in the mornings. This one strategy could be a game-changer for you. Try it for a week and see what happens.

If you can't put your phone down, I get it. You can still use your devices to *help* you sleep. For example, why not listen to sleep stories or meditations? If you tend to contemplate and think repetitive thoughts in bed, sleep stories could be helpful because they are written and read to transport your mind to a softer, calmer place. The spoken word and background music are designed to lower your brain's levels of the stress hormone cortisol. Some favorites of my students and friends are Calm sleep stories, sleep meditations from headspace.com, and the free *Sleepy Time* podcast. (And *try* not to look at the screen once you hit play.)

Whatever you choose, don't forget to also put your phone in "Do Not Disturb" or "Airplane Mode." You don't want any dings, vibrations, or light-up-the-screen alerts to disrupt your sleep. You are creating a personalized sun and moon schedule by turning your technology off—or at least way, way down.

You could also look into getting blue-light blocker glasses. Nonprescription versions usually aren't very expensive. (Or, if you wear prescription glasses, you can add a blue-light blocker to the lenses.) They help shut out those blue rays that tell your brain to power up just when you're trying to power down.

According to *Eat Move Sleep*, you may also sleep better if you can drop the temperature by two to four degrees each night before you get in bed, or trade heavier blankets for lighter ones. Think back to those early hunter-gatherers again. Exposure to the sun during the day naturally meant a warmer temperature. At night, cooler temps sent another signal to the ancient brain that it was time for some shut-eye. Research has shown that a slight drop in body temperature helps induce your body into a sleep state. Being a little colder in bed could help you fall asleep faster and sleep sounder than you would at your average room temperature. If you aren't able to change the temperature in your home, you could crack open a nearby window if it's cooler outside, turn on a ceiling fan if you have one, or put a small fan by your bed.

Lastly, aromatherapy helps some people sleep. Lavender, in particular, can soothe your muscles and your nervous system, so you might want to try using a diffuser or spraying a lavender mist on your sheets. As you inhale the calming scent, you can also do a breathing exercise for sleep preparation called the 4-4-6 method:

- 4: Breathe in through your nose for four seconds.
- 4: Hold the breath for four seconds.
- 6: Breathe out through your nose for six seconds.

Doing this practice, even for just two minutes, can calm your body and mind and prepare you for a good night's rest.

EXERCISE

Exercising during the day can help you sleep better at night. But if you're anything like me, there are probably days when you feel too busy or too tired to work out. What I've noticed, though, is that there is typically a very clear trade-off. If I can find 30 minutes to exercise during the day, I fall asleep almost immediately after getting in bed and sleep soundly throughout the night. If I *don't* exercise, I end up tossing and turning for up to an hour at night, and I don't feel as well-rested when I wake up the next day.

So on days where your schedule is packed, or you're coasting on fumes, try reminding yourself of this. Tell yourself, *If I can exercise for just 30 minutes today, I will probably sleep longer and better the whole night, and I won't have to feel like this tomorrow.*

It doesn't have to be an intense workout. Maybe you can turn on a favorite playlist and do push-ups and sit-ups when you get home from school or work. Or you could try jogging around your schoolyard during a free period, or ask someone to take a walk with you after dinner. The important thing is that you're moving. And during the day, movement is what matters, because it brings your spirit into stillness at night.

EATING HABITS

While breakfast and lunch directly impact your day, your evening meal and any snacks or drinks after that greatly influence your night. So before going to bed, try to avoid eating sugary foods or drinking anything that contains caffeine. Instead, stick with water or caffeine-free tea so you can fall asleep faster.

ENJOYING YOUR REWARD

Sleep is not a chore like cleaning the toilet, doing the dishes, or taking out the trash. It is a reward you earn for your hard work each day. So try to adopt the mindset that it's something to get excited about! Something to experience. Something to relax into. A break from the physical and mental jockeying between classes, clubs, and social events, and from all the social pressure and anxiety you might feel from teachers, parents, and peers. And it will give you the strength to keep fighting the good fight the next day—and fend off the Zombie Student who might be lurking within you!

CHAPTER **8**

CREATE A PERSONAL CREED

"The Inner Path" section of this book opened with creating a vision and building your vision board. And in this chapter, it ends with information about creating a personal creed—a set of values you can commit to living by, no matter the circumstances.

How is it all connected? Good question. Think of your vision board as a map with big red Xs that mark the important spots. These are some of the treasure chests you can discover as you travel.

And the creed? The creed is like a compass, a map, and a navigation app all in one. It will direct you safely and securely toward (and maybe even beyond) your goals, all while honoring your true self and values.

After all, it's not enough to know your end location while driving somewhere; you also have to know your way around potential roadblocks, traffic stops, and potholes that could slow you down or steer you off course. That's where a creed can help. It gathers the values you live by and lists them in a memorable way. It prepares you for how you will react to problems before they happen. It sharpens your behavior while you navigate.

And a creed can do even more. It can be especially valuable for anyone experiencing mental or physical illness, from depression or anxiety to chronic physical pain. A personal creed is a tool that you can use to tap into something called Acceptance and Commitment Therapy, commonly referred to as ACT. Created by Steven Hayes in 1982, this therapeutic treatment essentially begins with accepting whatever hand you've been dealt, and follows up with taking strategic action despite the adversity. That means accepting the reality of illness, pain, distress, or discomfort. It also means accepting the emotions attached to these challenges—like frustration, hopelessness, and anger—without suppressing any of them. But the process doesn't stop there. Next comes a critical step. You ask yourself, "Now that I have this inescapable pain, what *can* I do with it? How *can* I still move forward in life?"

Taking an ACT approach to your life is powerful. For trailblazers, denying reality is a form of retreat. But accepting it is the beginning of an advance into your future.

Your creed can help you do this. It reminds you of what really matters to you—whether in spite of or because of the challenges you face. And it points you in the direction of a life that matches up with those values.

WHAT DOES A PERSONAL CREED LOOK LIKE?

As Sean Covey points out in *The 7 Habits of Highly Effective Teens*, a mistake some teens make is trying to make a personal creed look just like someone else's. This can decrease your motivation to follow it because it's like you're living someone else's life rather than blazing your own trail.

Still, it may be hard to know where to start. If you need a little help, read on for a few questions, a visual to help you get going, and a pair of creed samples to help you brainstorm. Most of all, remember that your personal creed should still be just that—*personal*. It can come in many forms—a few words, a paragraph, a numbered list of principles, or even a song. This is *your* creed; you are the only one who gets to live it, so write it your way.

CONSTRUCTING YOUR PERSONAL CREED

The best starting point for your creed is to identify and evaluate your core values. From these, you can build mantras, and those mantras will form the basis of your creed.

What exactly is a value? Is it like a New Year's Resolution or a goal? As *The Depression Guidebook* (part of the Therapy Notebooks series) points out, "Values are different from goals because while a goal can be met or checked off, living your values is a consistent practice that guides behavior on an ongoing basis. For instance, if you have the value of 'justice,' then your actions will continually be guided by choices that help you seek and promote justice in your life." Basically, goals might guide your decision-making for a year, but values can guide you for a lifetime.

To get thinking about your values, check out the list of values on the next page. Which ones speak to you? Which ones resonate in your heart?

Choose your top four to eight values based on what is most important to you—for your past, present, and future. Write them in a notebook, on your phone, or wherever you like. And if you think of any that aren't listed here, feel free to add them.

- Acceptance
- Adventure
- Altruism
- Athleticism
- Competition
- Courage
- Creativity
- Education
- Empathy
- Family
- Fun
- Gratitude
- Humility
- Humor
- Innovation
- Integrity
- Intimacy
- Joy
- Justice
- Leadership
- Loving-kindness
- Order
- Peace
- Play
- Self-Care
- Service
- Spirituality

Now that you've given some thought to your core values, you can ensure they remain a guiding light on your journey by using them to write mantras—short, hard-to-forget statements that you can recall and repeat when you need them. Try to write one mantra for each value you chose. For instance, if you identified creativity as one of your values, the related mantra could be, "I treasure my creative spirit."

If it helps you to have a visual reference, you could even place your mantras into a symbolic compass, as in the following example. Then you can build on this framework to put together your creed. If you like, you can also keep your compass in a daily planner, place it in a picture frame, or put it on your vision board as a reminder of your values and your commitment to living by them every day. You can download a compass template at go.freespirit.com/blaze or from the "free stuff" section of my website, justinfashley.com.

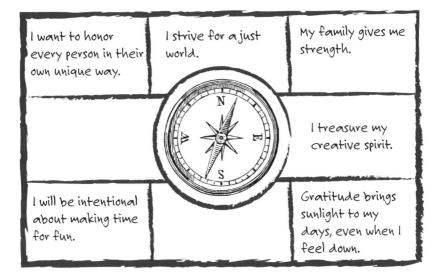

I want to honor every person in their own unique way.

I strive for a just world.

My family gives me strength.

I treasure my creative spirit.

I will be intentional about making time for fun.

Gratitude brings sunlight to my days, even when I feel down.

To further personalize your values and develop your mantras, consider your answers to these four questions for each value you chose from the list:

1. **WHAT IS MY STYLE?** Your style is about how you present yourself to the world, and while it can include things like what you wear and what music you like, it goes deeper too. What parts of your style help you feel most authentic to yourself? How does your style reflect your identity?

2. **WHAT DO I ENJOY DOING MOST?** Think about things you do that don't feel like work, where you lose your sense of time and place. What excites you or inspires you?

3. **WHAT DO I WANT PEOPLE TO SAY ABOUT ME WHILE I'M ALIVE?** How do you want others to describe you when you're not around and your

name comes up in conversation? This could especially apply to the people you care most about—the ones in your inner circle, like your closest classmates, teachers, family members, and friends. Think about the qualities that are important to you that you hope they see.

4. **WHAT LEGACY DO I WANT TO LEAVE IN THIS WORLD?** It may be scary to think about death, but there's no escaping it. It's part of the human experience. So think about what you'd want people to say about you after you die and what you hope will live on because you were here—what you can leave behind even after you're gone. Then you can begin building your legacy as you live.

Okay: You have your values and your mantras. Now it's time to put it all together. Here are two samples of creeds that might further inspire you and give you more ideas for your own. First, here's mine:

I smile each day, even after the darkest of nights.
I bring the fun to the party.
I boast about others, not myself.
I maintain a quiet confidence.
I seek wisdom.
I am an adventurer and an explorer.
I take ownership.
I make solutions, not excuses.
I turn up the voices that matter around me and mute the ones that don't.
I am an extreme achiever.
I place scholarship above social obligation, success above convenience,
and character above appearance.
I seek to be loving rather than popular.
I speak kindly, act sincerely, and choose thoughtfully.
When my life in this world comes to an end,
I will die empty and full.

Empty because I've given all I could to my family,
friends, students, and passions.
Full because I've fulfilled God's calling on my life.

After reading my creed, can you guess some of my core principles?
You got it if you thought: adventure, education, fun, joy, loving-kindness,
service, spirituality, or wisdom.

And here's a personal creed written by a teen named Declan Wagner
Bielicki:

I ask myself, often, if what I am doing is fun.
Because what is a life lived without joy?
What is a life lived without bursting laughter and the innocence of a smile?
Laughter, in nature, is contagious
He who laughs will spark others to do the same
And those who do not, he can steer clear of
Malice is the product of doubt, sorrow, and fear
Laughter in malice is laughter without integrity
And without integrity, there is no peace
If I cannot be honest with myself, I cannot be honest with anyone else
If I cannot have integrity, I cannot have peace
And so I apply this to those around me, through two sides of a coin:
Humor, wit, charm, and lighthearted enjoyment
Alongside honesty, truth, trust, and understanding.
I live in the former half as much as I can;
I live in color, in creativity, in ideas and dreams as much as I can
But I know I cannot provide a foundation for my dreams without integrity
Without the brutally honest and the silencing talks
Without the "Please just listen" and the "I'm here for whatever you need"
People know me for my sincerity and my energy
For my ability to drop everything and listen wholeheartedly when needed

And for my tendency to drive them to the teetering edge of annoyed
Only to seek my presence once more
Because what's a little annoyance if you're having fun?
We could all learn to live life just a bit more freely
With wide eyes rather than turned heads
With the question of "Why?" rather than a raised nose
Perhaps, not unlike that of a child, brimming with wonder.
So when I die and someone asks what I was known for,
The response may be some achievement of mine
A book, a tournament medal, a title
More likely, however, it will be the light I aim to bring as I walk into a room
Not to try and blind those around me
But with the intent of lighting the candle everyone else holds
Especially those who simply need a little spark to set theirs alight.

WHAT NEXT?

It might take a few tries to get your creed right. It's not a contest, and it's not a race. What matters is that you end up with something that feels good and true to *you*. When you read it, you feel proud and inspired, and it fills you with hope and confidence.

Once you've created your creed, place it somewhere you'll see it often: perhaps near your vision board, on your nightstand, tucked into a daily planner, or on your refrigerator. I read mine aloud in the mornings before starting each day, and I have it memorized by now. When I screw up at school or home, I remember to take ownership and try to make it right. When I don't sleep well at night and feel grumpy the following day, I remind myself that I'm a joyful person: *I smile each day, even after the darkest of nights.*

Creating your creed is an opportunity to crystallize your values and goals and to practice living by them—progressing through life with meaning, and leaning into your inner voice of conviction. By writing, reading, rereading, and repeating this creed, your values and mantras will become wired into your long-term memory. And when that happens, they can pop up in your mind at opportune moments and nudge you to take action.

- If one of your values is *service*, you might find purpose in volunteering at organizations that serve people, animals, or the environment.

- If a value of yours is *self-care*, you could discover meaning in a counseling session or by doing something that brings you personal satisfaction, like drawing, painting, journaling, or woodworking.

- If you value *intimacy*, you might find significance in writing and sending personal letters to loved ones, planning romantic dates, or opening up to your friends and being vulnerable by sharing your true feelings, fears, and desires.

- If one of your values is *athleticism*, you could feel empowered by studying your favorite sport and not just playing it. You might read books and articles about it, watch training videos online, and develop new ways to improve your game. For example, some professional basketball and football players have committed to yoga, water aerobics, and ballet to improve their footwork.

This action step is important. Because while a creed can give us a guide to move in a specific direction, we also have to follow through. I know it's hard sometimes, but it's essential to commit. *Commitment:* that's the *C* in ACT. Without it, you will stay where you're AT, but with it, you can take ACTion. (I'm not sure if that's what Dr. Hayes was going for with his acronym, but I say we run with it.) Accepting your struggles and clarifying your values and purpose get you part of the way. Commitment and action take you to the next level.

LOOKING AHEAD

Before you begin the next section, "The Outer Path," and the third section, "The Onward Path," know there is rugged terrain ahead. Pioneering isn't easy. I know sometimes it might feel like this path leads you through a night where your only company is the stars above and unknown creatures growling in the bushes around you.

Maybe it feels like forging through a storm. Or perhaps it feels like running up a hill that you can't see over. But when you're tempted to turn back, take it one step at a time and lean on your creed. The struggles will be worth it if you prepare yourself for problems and stay true to your character.

When you encounter those dark nights, those storms and hills, how will you respond? Your creed is powerful because it answers that question in advance and keeps you moving forward with purpose, conviction, and passion. The fog will clear, the darkness will fade, and the light will shine through.

PART TWO
THE OUTER PATH

CHAPTER 9

FORM YOUR SQUAD

Suppose a friend makes a joke on Snapchat that hurts your feelings. An irritable teacher snaps at you in front of the whole class. A stranger bumps into you at the movie theater, rolls their eyes, and makes a rude comment. A family member teases you.

What happens with those words? A lot of times, we begin to repeat them in our minds—and even turn up the volume. We remember them, over and over again. This is called *ruminating*, and it's a dangerous type of thinking. In time, it can lead to low self-esteem, anxiety, and depression.

The good news is that you can stop replaying what the critics and gossips say about you on Instagram, on TikTok, on sports fields, in your neighborhood, and at home. You can instead begin to listen to the kinder voices in your life. How? By forming a squad—a Teen Squad, made just for you:

1. Take a sticky note, index card, or small piece of paper. Draw a straight line from top to bottom and another across the middle, creating four squares, or four rectangles within a rectangle.

2. Label the first box Family. Label the second box Friends. Title the third box Personal Mentors, and the fourth Public Voices.

3. Next, write down the names of the most influential people in your life for each category. These are the ones who have earned your trust or given you positive vibes:

   a. Family members such as parents, grandparents, siblings, cousins, aunts, and uncles

   b. Friends at school; around your neighborhood; in a club, theater, or performance group; on a team; or at work

   c. Personal mentors including teachers, principals, counselors, therapists, coaches, trainers, or spiritual leaders

   d. Public voices you admire, like your favorite authors, artists, musicians, athletes, activists, or other figures. You won't know these people in real life, but that doesn't mean they can't be role models for you.

4. Put this list somewhere close at hand. Maybe it's hidden on the inside cover of your planner or a notebook. Or you could tuck it into your wallet or phone case.

5. Next time you're stuck thinking about something someone said about you, take a look at your list. Is the person who did the talking in any of those four squares? (In the case of the public voices section, these folks probably won't be talking about you, specifically. But the loud voices in the world can still say things that feel hurtful, because we relate to them or apply them to ourselves.) If they aren't, forget what they said. If they are, listen to the feedback. If it's positive, replay it. Revel in it. Turn up the volume on it.

If the feedback is critical, take a closer look at it. Be honest with yourself and see what you can learn from it, and if it can help you grow. Even replay it if you need to, to take what you need—but just once or twice.

TRUE TO HER NAME

Here's a story of someone who had multiple voices to choose from. In 1997, a girl named Malala Yousafzai was born in Pakistan's Swat District. Her father, Ziauddin, was an educator who opened a small school for boys *and* girls—including Malala. In the classroom and at home, he would encourage her, affirming that her voice mattered and that she should share her thoughts aloud.

However, other voices in Malala's world said otherwise. Her family's life was turned upside-down when members of the Taliban—an extremist political and religious group—gained control of the Swat Valley in 2007. The Taliban believed it was a violation of their interpretation of Islam for girls to be educated. They began bombing schools where girls were enrolled. Nevertheless, as a teenager, Malala drew upon her father's encouragement and his passion for education. She summoned her courage and publicly spoke out against the Taliban, saying they had no right to stop her from learning.

Then, in 2012, Malala and some of her classmates were on their way home from school when Taliban terrorists boarded their bus. After asking which of the girls was Malala, they opened fire and shot her in the head. Amazingly, she made a full recovery. Rather than let the experience silence her, she went on to speak even louder for girls around the world. Along with her father, she founded the Malala Fund in 2014, dedicated to helping girls achieve education and define their own futures. That same year, at age 17, she became the youngest recipient of the Nobel Peace Prize. In 2015, to celebrate her 18th birthday, she opened a school for Syrian refugee girls in Lebanon. In 2017, she traveled to Nigeria to speak up on behalf of girls there who could not go to school because of an extremist group known as Boko Haram. And her work goes on today.

Clearly, Malala had the ability and the courage to turn up the volume on the positive voices in her life and turn down the harmful and negative ones. In a way, this began even before she was born. In her book *I Am Malala,* she explains that beginning when she was in her mother's belly, her father spoke to her in an inspiring voice. He would tell and retell the story of Malalai, a teenage girl who was said to have gone into battle during the Second Anglo-Afghan War in 1880, when the English were invading Afghanistan.

The Afghans were losing the battle and retreating. When Malalai saw the flag bearer fall to the ground, she headed onto the battlefield herself, shouting to the soldiers, "Young love! If you do not fall in the battle . . . then, by God, someone is saving you as a symbol of shame." The soldiers followed her lead, returned to fight, and won the battle.

Though Malalai died in the battle, Ziauddin named his daughter after this warrior and told her the story not to teach her about death, but about courage. In a sense, he was whispering: *You will be brave. You will be strong. You will be fearless. You will be a trailblazer.* She listened to and lived by that voice her whole life, and she continues to do so today. She lives a life true to her name.

But what if? What if she had listened to the many voices telling her she should be silent? Telling her she didn't deserve an education? What if she had replayed the Taliban's voice, rather than her father's? It's impossible to say how many girls' lives would be changed as a result.

I truly believe that the same ideas apply to you—and to all of us. If you allow your mind to replay past words from the wrong voices, those same voices gain the power to dictate your future. But if you are able to listen to and replay the helpful voices that give you support, courage, and energy, *you* begin to dictate your future.

I get it if you're thinking that this process sounds both overly simple and too challenging at the same time. And I'll admit that it takes practice. But I can report from experience that it works! I've used it when I've heard other teachers criticizing me at school and when I've read negative comments about me online. And I'm certainly not the only one who's figured this secret out. Many of my students have told me they've used it too, with a lot of success. It's liberating because it helps you set aside toxicity and replace it with positivity.

No matter what your critics and the cynics are saying about you, you can rise above it. But to do so, you've got to start turning up the volume on the voices that really matter to you and muting those that don't. Take charge of your remote control. Stop spending energy trying to get everyone's approval or follow the norm, and instead focus on what the people most important to you are saying.

PATTERN RECOGNITION

A question I sometimes get about the Teen Squad is, "What if a person on my list says something negative or critical about me?"

My first answer would be to take another look at step 5 in the directions for forming your squad. It'll give you ideas about what to do when someone in your squad offers something other than praise. But here's another piece of advice: Look for patterns in feedback. If one of your favorite teachers makes a sarcastic or dismissive comment to you offhand, that can hurt. But it's one comment, on one day. The teacher might have had a bad week or could be dealing with something you don't know about. It doesn't mean they should have said what they did—and hopefully they'll realize this and even apologize. In any case, if their comment doesn't match the way they usually treat you, try to view it as an oddity that doesn't demand your full attention (or top volume in your brain).

On the other hand, if multiple teachers you admire say you're not performing to your full potential, and you notice your grades dropping, and your parents tell you that you're playing too many video games, *and* a friend asks you to be quiet during a lesson because it's distracting you both . . . well, then you have multiple pieces of evidence suggesting you might need to up your educational game.

Your Teen Squad will often affirm that you are on the right path. Other times, they will try to nudge you back on course. Both come from a place of love, and both deserve a listening ear.

CHAPTER 10

LEARN TO ACCEPT WHAT YOU'RE SERVED AT THE FEEDBACK DINER

We've all received critical feedback from authority figures in our lives, whether at school, at home, on a team, or at a job.

Frustration with feedback is normal. And often, the most disappointing part isn't the feedback itself; it's how the input is delivered that really fires us up.

It might have been delivered at the wrong location: "Did she have to call me out in front of the whole team? Why not address this quietly on the sideline or talk to me alone after the game?"

Or it could be delivered at the wrong time: "It's Friday. I have had practice and homework every night this week. I'm exhausted. And now my dad wants to yell at me because my room is messy. Really?"

Or it's delivered by the wrong person: "This new teacher barely even knows me. Plus, she's just a few years older than I am, and she's no expert. How can she give me a C on this when I know I deserve an A?"

When this happens, it's common for us to quickly dismiss what was said because of when and where we received it and who we received it from. We don't want to chew on the feedback and swallow it down. Instead, we choke. We get angry. But choking every time you eat only means you will starve to death. Anyone who wants to grow into greatness has to learn to take in feedback—to chew, swallow, and digest it.

So this is the path forward: Every time you get feedback, pretend you're eating at a restaurant where feedback is the main course. And the people giving you that feedback might be the restaurant owners, cooks, or servers. They run the kitchen. They're in control, to a degree. But it's still up to you to get the most out of your meal.

UNDERSTAND THE FOOD ON THE MENU

In *Thanks for the Feedback*, Harvard lecturers Douglas Stone and Sheila Heen suggest identifying the feedback before you try to process it. They cite three types: appreciation (thank you for doing that), evaluation (this is where you stand right now), and coaching (instead of doing that, do this next time).

We need each type of feedback to grow stronger throughout our lives. Appreciation-style feedback from a teacher or coach, like, "That presentation you gave in class was powerful," or "I appreciate you stepping up when our team needed you in the game," could lift your spirits and self-esteem. There are also times when you need coaching, like when you get into a fight with a best friend and are entirely out of ideas for a resolution. In other moments you may need to hear evaluation, such as the honest assessment that your social media use has gotten out of control.

Sometimes I think we expect to be served our absolute favorite meal every single day. Say it's tasty chicken tenders and fries—something like, "Thanks for working so hard. I'm so proud of you. You are brilliant and amazing." Instead, some days we get a "You can do better!" salad with a bitter vinaigrette. It's not the feedback we're hungry for. But the feedback we don't want to swallow is often the feedback that's most important for us to take in.

It's also important to keep in mind how tough it is for the kitchen to send out the just-right serving of feedback. After all, just like you, they are busy, flawed people. They are trying to serve other customers at the same time—whether those are siblings, classmates, teammates, or coworkers. The Feedback Diner is a packed restaurant with a 30-minute wait, and you scored a reservation. So when your meal arrives, it's a good idea to take it in and do something with it. To be grateful for it. Even if it's not what you crave at that moment, it's what people you trust feel you need.

No matter what dish ends up in front of us, we can use each type of feedback to our advantage in some way. Appreciation helps us realize we are making a difference in the lives of others. Coaching helps us become better and raises us to a higher standard. Evaluation gives us an insider's expert assessment of our skills or performance. To help you swallow the dish that's being offered, ask yourself these questions:

- What type of feedback was I expecting or hoping for? Appreciation? Coaching? Evaluation?
- What type of feedback am I being served today? Appreciation? Coaching? Evaluation?
- Do I need to realign my expectations so that I can digest the feedback I've been given?

If your teacher called you up to their desk or your mom called you on the phone and you didn't get the type of feedback you expected or wanted, that takes a mental shift. To see the feedback for what it is and use it wisely, try the suggestions in the next sections.

CHANGE HOW YOU CHEW

The way you'd eat a salmon dinner is different from how you'd eat an ice cream cone. One needs a knife and fork; the other requires . . . well, a lot of licking. Similarly, different types of feedback require different responses.

A lot of the time, leaders at home, at school, in sports, and elsewhere can rely *too* much on the coaching and evaluation styles of feedback. But appreciation is just as critical. The appreciation sort of feedback is usually what we love to hear. It's the sweet stuff. It could be a shout-out in the locker room or a roaring round of applause after a performance. Or it could be affirmative words a teacher wrote on your essay, or your dad telling how proud he is of you.

When you get positive feedback, try to extend its impact beyond the moment you receive it. You could record it in your notes app on your phone so you can remind yourself of what the person said. If it arrives via a text,

DM, or comment on social media, you could save a screenshot of it. If it's an email, you can print it out, or if it's a thank-you card, you might hang it up somewhere so you can revisit it when you need a boost.

Figuring out what to do with coaching and evaluation can be more difficult, partly because accepting these forms of feedback requires recognizing that you are imperfect—and that can leave a nasty aftertaste. Feeling offended, disappointed, or overwhelmed when facing constructive criticism is natural, but try not to get tangled up with emotions. Keep your cool. Don't yell. Don't send the meal back to the kitchen—or flip the table in a rage.

Instead, think logically about one thing you can do with the feedback immediately after the conversation. Then, whatever that one thing is, respond with a verbal commitment: *This is what I hear from you. This is what I'm going to do today, tomorrow, and the next day.* It could be something simple. If your teacher says you earned a D on an essay, commit to attending a writing tutoring session during your free period at least once a week, and ask if the teacher has other suggestions to help you improve. If your coach says you are slower than your opponents, promise to do fifty lunges every day to build your leg strength and get faster, and ask if there is anything else they would suggest. If your parent is concerned about how long you are gaming each day, promise them you will set a timer for an hour and stop gaming for the day when it goes off. Show them you are committed to the process. You may not be able to figure out everything at once, but you can at least do one thing. And that's all it takes to show a leader in your life that giving you feedback was worth their effort.

It may also help you accept feedback if you can remember that the person giving it is not evaluating you as a person or trying to define (or damage) your self-worth. Instead, they are assessing your behavior or performance, telling you how you're doing, and offering their unique perspective on how you can do better.

SORTING OUT THE JUST-PLAIN-CRITICS FROM THE CONSTRUCTIVE CRITICS

It might sound counterintuitive, but I think that sometimes, subconsciously, we seek out critics. It's almost like we want people to tell us we can't accomplish something just so we can prove them wrong.

That can be good fuel for the mind and body. But the best fuel often comes from your teachers, coaches, and family members—the people who don't just offer criticism, but *constructive* criticism. They care about you. They want you to succeed. And they want to help you get there, even when it requires uncomfortable conversations.

If you're willing to listen, these people can offer greater insight than some casual acquaintance or anonymous troll online. That's because their feedback comes from a place of love, experience, and vision. They are trying to give you advice based on their experience and expertise. Sometimes it's humbling. Sometimes it hurts. But it may be necessary to take you to your next level. Let's dig deeper by looking at each of the previous examples of coaching and evaluation statements and seeing how they could be meant for your benefit, even if you're not wild about hearing them.

Your essay earned a D because it doesn't meet the criteria I clearly explained. Earlier in the school year, this teacher has seen you crush it as a writer. They know your potential and want you to be able to reach the pinnacle, communicate clearly, and follow directions when you begin a career one day.

You are slower than your opponents. You have the natural talent to be elite in your sport, but your lack of leg strength is holding you back. Your coach wants you to learn how to work hard, earn that medal, and maybe even be awarded a college scholarship.

You are playing too many video games. Your parent might have been playing Nintendo, Sega, and PlayStation 1 at your age. Maybe they look back and feel like they wasted time and potential trying to save Princess Peach from Bowser's castle when they could have been playing outside or spending quality time with friends. They don't want you to grow up with the same regrets.

So don't just prove your critics wrong. Prove your constructive critics right. Digest their feedback and let it help you move ahead toward bigger and better things.

IF THE FOOD LOOKS BAD, GET A SECOND OPINION

You wouldn't bite into a piece of moldy bread. Questionable advice is no different. If it doesn't feel right—if there is a deeper kind of unease beyond the initial sting—get a second opinion.

Talk to another authority figure or best friend—someone who cares about you and whom you can trust to be authentic. Start with something like, "This is how my teacher told me I should have handled the situation differently. I feel like I did the right thing. What do you think?"

Sometimes, you might realize you were overreacting to the feedback in the moment, and that you needed a little distance and an outside viewpoint. Other times, you may find truth in your gut feeling. Like old food in the back of the pantry, the advice that felt wrong could be outdated or expired. Or it might just not be right for *you*. In this case, it may be best to toss the feedback aside—or to ask for clarification from the person who gave it to you.

ORDER UP

So: You're sitting at the Feedback Diner, and your circle of mentors have prepared a meal for you. What will you do next? Will you choke or chew? Sometimes we don't chew, and sometimes we refuse to swallow. Either way, we starve our body and our spirit of what we need to function and grow.

Receiving feedback is hard work, and it takes humility and selflessness. It's an acquired taste. But consider this: teens who choke on the feedback they need could end up going hungry while waiting for the food they desire. On the flip side, teens who are able to chew on, swallow, and digest words from their parents, teachers, and coaches can benefit from the wisdom within, allowing them to be healthier, happier, and more successful human beings. So take a look at the menu. What will you choose?

CHAPTER 11

TAKE MINI-ADVENTURES WITH FAMILY AND FRIENDS

Several years ago, my wife, Samantha, and I were going through a very rough time. In fact, we were considering getting a divorce. But first, we committed to taking short weekend field trips with our son, Cole, to bring some fun back to our family.

One of those trips was to DuPont Recreational State Forest, near Asheville, North Carolina, where several scenes from one of our favorite movies, *The Hunger Games*, were filmed. One of the spots we wanted to make it to is situated near the top of three waterfalls. Called Triple Falls, it's the backdrop of a charming fictional moment in a gorgeous real-life location.

We parked our car, hiked up a few miles to the bottom of the top waterfall, and quickly recognized the spot from the film. The sound of the water above colliding with the rocks and river below was so soothing. We sat down and took in the scene for a few minutes. Then, we snapped a few family pictures.

There was a small whirlpool nearby, and I got the idea to tiptoe near that water to feel how cold it was. I bent down at the edge to touch the water and slipped on slick rock, falling into the whirlpool. The water was freezing! I tried to swim back toward my family, but the momentum was against me, pushing me into the main current of the stream. I was heading toward a near-certain death, as the drop of the second waterfall was just ahead of me.

To make matters worse, my son, who was four years old, panicked and jumped into the water to save his dad. Cole didn't know how to swim, so my wife, who was five months pregnant at the time, dove in to save us both. Now, we were all about to die in the Hunger Games arena.

Luckily, just before the drop, the water was shallow. I found my footing on the ground and pushed myself toward my son. My wife and I met him there, scooped him up, and swam back to the side of the stream. We were shivering and out of breath, but we were together and alive. We walked back down that mountain together, holding hands with connected spirits. We felt so much more love and gratitude on our way down than walking up. That waterfall changed us. It was as if a string had been threaded through our hearts, pulling us together.

It's a dangerous, scary story, but our son still talks about this as one of the great adventures in his life. I feel the same way. Do you know what we don't talk about? Do you know what story doesn't resonate with us all, years later? The weekend before, when I was doing schoolwork, he was watching

TV. Pretty mundane. Not very memorable or enjoyable, and certainly not adventurous.

We all want to escape the monotony of our environments from time to time. Being travelers is within our DNA, and we need awe and exploration to discover new sights, sounds, and smells. After reading this chapter, please don't go cannonballing into a waterfall. But consider taking a mini-adventure—breaking free from your usual surroundings to do a little (safe) exploring.

This doesn't have to be spontaneous, either—you can plan it out. In my household, we plan Family and Friend Field Trips, and we embrace lykke (pronounced LOO-kah), the Danish belief that happiness is everywhere around you if you are willing to get out and find it. You can read more about this idea at the end of this chapter. But for now, here are some tips to help you plan your own mini-adventures and pursue this idea.

1. **MAKE A LIST OF FAMILY AND FRIENDS.** Jot down names of people in your inner circle you'd like to travel with: parents, siblings, cousins, aunts and uncles, teammates, club members, neighborhood friends, and friends from school. You could take a look at your Teen Squad list from chapter 9 to help you get this list started.

2. **MAKE A MINI-ADVENTURE WISH LIST.** Create a list of places you want to go by yourself or with a few people from step 1. If you want a template for this, you can download one at go.freespirit.com/ blaze or from the "free stuff" section of my website, justinfashley. com. Or you can just jot down a list on your phone, in a journal, or however works for you. Either way, take a deep dive with this—talk to people who've visited these spots, check out websites, read reviews online, and call places you're interested in. Try to come up with at least 24 ideas. Depending on where you live and what forms of transportation you have available, also set a maximum

distance from your home. Setting a time limit on travel will help you keep the cost down. Some of these trips can even be close to free. In fact, some of my family's favorite trips, and some of the field trips where my students have had the most fun, have been to destinations that were free or cheap to visit.

Need help with ideas? Here are a few teen favorites based on what I've observed. You could:

→ Play retro and new games at an arcade.

→ Go ice skating.

→ Go ghost hunting in graveyards.

→ Take a ghost tour in a historical city.

→ Ride bikes on city streets or nature trails.

→ Play frisbee at a park or a beach.

→ Find some free outdoor music.

→ Go rock climbing.

→ Go zip lining.

→ Fish off a pier.

→ Play in paintball battles.

→ Arrange a scavenger hunt.

→ Compete in a laser tag game.

→ Race go-karts.

→ Take sketchbooks to a coffee shop, museum, park—anywhere you want—and draw the most interesting thing you see.

→ Sing karaoke.

→ Play dodgeball (and if you want to take this to the next level, try playing it at a trampoline park).

→ Learn to skateboard—or teach someone else.

→ Spend a day volunteering at a food bank or animal shelter.

→ Tour a historical site.

→ Try to win at a trivia night.

→ Go bowling.

→ Ride roller coasters.

→ Break out of escape rooms.

→ Go snow tubing.

→ Make a funny music video.

And this is only the beginning! Search online or talk to friends and family to come up with other ideas. Before long, you'll be living it up and exploring brand-new experiences.

3. **KEEP YOUR PLAN VISIBLE.** In *The Happiness Advantage*, Shawn Achor references a study based on positive psychology, where participants who thought about watching a favorite movie raised their levels of endorphin, a happiness booster in the brain, by 27 percent—just by *thinking* about the film! Similarly, you can lift your spirits by seeing your mini-adventure list. It can remind you of a favorite trip you've already taken or one you're looking forward to. You could create a slideshow and keep it on your computer desktop or your phone's favorites screen. Place a paper plan by your bed, your desk, your mirror—anywhere that works for you, so long as you'll see it often.

   Once you have specific dates for trips, you can also add these to your school schedule or monthly digital calendar. As you are writing down your homework for the week or planning out your school week filled with tests, you might feel overwhelmed, but then you come across a reminder of your trip on Saturday, which could create a spark of excitement.

4. **MAKE MINI-ADVENTURES A REGULAR ROUTINE, NOT A SPECIAL OCCASION.** Commit to a regular excursion, depending on what's manageable for you and your travel partners. That could be every weekend, once a month, or a couple of times per season. The goal is not to take all 24 trips in a year. It's to get into a rhythm of wandering into the unknown with people whose company you enjoy. That's the Outer Journey. It's braving the elements, but not alone. Family and friends make it more comforting, memorable, and joyful.

ANSWERING THE "WHAT-IF" QUESTIONS

Even if you take all the steps you've just read about, you might still have some questions about how to put your plans into action. You might be asking a lot of "what-ifs." Here are some ideas to help with those.

What If I'm an Introvert?

Try pairing a family-or-friends excursion with a solo outing.

If you're introverted, it may feel difficult or unnatural to lead or plan a trip with others. So try to have faith that you'll find some joy in it, and then *also* pencil down a solo activity for yourself the next day, weekend, or month as a reward for stepping out of your comfort zone. It's like advancing and retreating, pushing your way forward and then pulling back to recover. I'm an introvert too. It's not that we don't like being around people, but we also highly value and prefer time for ourselves—reading, writing, painting, resting—so do both.

Find a quiet spot someplace—inside or out—where you can lose yourself in a book. Go for a long walk or shoot some hoops on your own. Pick a pleasant spot to listen to your favorite podcast or playlist, or just to hear the birds and feel the breeze. Make two field trip lists—one for friends and family and one for yourself.

What If I Don't Know How to Get Family and Friends to Join Me?

If your parents need convincing, try initiating a conversation and openly sharing your desires. In your own words, explain why you want to get out and do more with them and others. Maybe you feel disconnected and think these outings could be helpful for your well-being and for your family. You could even share your slideshow or paper plan with your parents to show you've done some prep work. And you could ask if there is some way you could earn this as a reward or receive it as a birthday or holiday gift.

Be sure to make it clear that these trips don't have to take a lot of time or money.

As for getting friends or other potential mini-adventure partners on board, you could begin by telling them about a trip you've been wanting to take. Maybe share some details about where you'd go, what you'd do there, why it would be fun—even what you'd eat. You could also show them a few pictures or videos of the spot. All of this could pique their interest and make them more open to joining you on an excursion. In addition, ask them about places they'd like to visit. Maybe they'll end up inviting you along on a mini-adventure of their own!

What If I Feel Too Anxious and Depressed to Go Out?

If you are afraid of loud noises, overwhelmed by large crowds, or sometimes feel so hopeless that you want to pull up the covers, turn on the TV, and stay in bed, I hear you. I've been there.

Something that's encouraged and energized me over the years is the Danish concept of lykke (pronounced LOO-kah), which I read about in *The Scandinavian Guide to Happiness*, a book by Tim Rayborn.

Lykke is the idea that happiness is everywhere around you. Based partly on this mentality, Danes have built a country that ranks consistently among the happiest on Earth. They spend a lot of time outdoors—at festivals, parks, concerts, sports, and swimming—even on rainy days. If you were to travel there right now, you might see more walkers and bikers than you do cars. It's a clean, green country with low rates of poverty, minimal crime, and free education and healthcare for all citizens. (This comes at a cost, of course: high taxes.)

Like the people of Denmark, you can try intentionally building this idea into your life over time. You can work on cultivating the belief that happiness is all around you, and then you can practice getting out and taking part in it. This begins with your networks. Through family and friend mini-adventures, you start connecting with people and experiences that make you *want* to rise out of bed each day, drown out the noises in those big crowds, and move forward.

For me, one thing that has helped is reminding myself that I could lie in that bed for as long I wanted, but my soul wouldn't feel at rest. I could binge-watch every season of my favorite TV show, but I wouldn't find genuine joy upon finishing it. When anxiety and depression have taken hold, I've often felt like I'm trapped—locked in an emotional prison. And one of the keys I've used to break out was lykke.

This doesn't happen all at once. It's hard work. You'll have ups and downs. And it's okay to ask for help. But doing the work is the tax worth paying. And the reward is in everyone and everything around you, patiently waiting for you to join in and be truly free. It's lykke.

CHAPTER 12

SET UP A STUDY SANCTUARY

Confession: I nearly failed out of college and lost a full scholarship after my first semester as a freshman at UNC Charlotte.

I needed a minimum of a 2.25 GPA to keep the North Carolina Teaching Fellows Scholarship I had been awarded. After a lot of partying, basketball, late-night video games, and wasted time, I earned a 2.24. Once the grades were posted in December, the dean of the College of Education called me into her office and told me she would give me one more semester to fix this, or I would lose my scholarship, which meant I would have to return home.

I needed solutions. My first problem was that the coursework was harder than it had been in high school, and to succeed I had to be fully engaged in class—which I wasn't. The second problem was the homework; I had become distracted by the social whirlwind of campus life. Not sure what else to do, I made an appointment to see a doctor on campus. She confirmed something I'd suspected for quite a while: I have ADHD. She prescribed medication that helped me turn my attention to the front of the lecture halls (and keep it there). But homework was still an issue.

I tried to go to our school's library, but there were usually a lot of people on the first three floors, and it was rarely quiet. Printers were printing. Librarians and students were talking. Friends and a girlfriend popped by my table to say hello. After several failed attempts to do my best work on those lower floors, I packed my bag up and headed to the elevator. I needed a quiet space, void of distraction.

I pressed the button for the fourth floor, and after the doors opened, I walked around to see if the atmosphere was different. Nope. Still too many people and too much noise. I repeated the test for the fifth, sixth, and seventh floors, with the same result. Then came the eighth floor. It was smaller and featured several shelves of old reference books, a few large tables and chairs in the center, desks lining the front and center of the room, and windows galore. I was so high in the sky I could see nearly the entire campus. And the best part? There was no one else there. Literally no one. It was just a bunch of books and me.

This floor became my academic utopia for the rest of that spring semester, and then for the rest of my college career. My own study sanctuary. Nearly every day after class, I headed up there (hoping no one would follow), turned off the lights, sat by a window, and broke open the books. By the end of the year, my GPA had risen from 2.24 to 3.5.

The following year, when I became the Scholarship Chair of my fraternity, I shared my secret with my brothers. The school required them to complete four hours of study hall per week in the library on the second floor. I increased it to six hours and instructed them to come to the Study Sanctuary on the eighth floor instead.

We were known as the "jock" fraternity, made up mostly of athletes and gym rats, and our cumulative GPA was the lowest out of all the frats on campus. But by the end of my sophomore year, we had the second-highest cumulative GPA. We were still athletes, and we had also become scholars. One of my brothers later told me he wouldn't have graduated college without the eighth floor. Looking back, I feel the same way.

Just one shift in location—just turning a dusty library floor into a sacred study space—can make all the difference. It did for my brothers and me, and it can for you too.

If you want to create a study sanctuary of your own, where your learning, exploration, and curiosity can take center stage, here are a few ideas, based on the five senses, that might help. And if you don't have complete control over your space or how you set it up, that's okay. We'll figure out some ways to work with what you've got.

SIGHT: ADJUST THE LIGHTING AND THE SCENERY

What do you prefer—a lot of light, a little light, or almost no light? You could use a bright desk lamp, move your desk to be near a window, or black out the room by using dark curtains to block the windows. Some students put dimmable, color-changing LED lights around their rooms.

To change the scenery, is there a peaceful picture you would love to put above or beside your desk, like a poster of Van Gogh's *The Starry Night*,

Hokusai's *The Great Wave off Kanagawa*, or Raphael's *The School of Athens*? Or maybe you could get an artificial or natural plant, like a pothos, spider plant, or African violet. (Ask around about spider plants if you know people who have a lot of houseplants. They send out offshoots that are easy to cut and replant.)

SMELL: LIGHT UP A UNIQUE SCENT

What's your favorite smell? Pumpkin? Cinnamon? Ocean air? Clean laundry? Froot Loops? There are candles, essential oils, and incenses for all these scents and more to help you make your sanctuary yours. Yes, even Froot Loops. I diffuse it in my classroom, and my students love it. You could even put a little bit of nice-smelling lotion on your hands, or keep a small glass of coffee beans nearby if that's a scent you love.

This may seem trivial, but it's important to be strategic about scents, because they can make or break the aura. The goal is to associate learning with as many positives as possible. Suppose you sit down to do calculus and smell dirty socks or a nasty odor from a clogged toilet nearby. You may immediately be turned off by the combination of a challenging task and an unpleasant scent, instead of being able to control your breath and relax into the task at hand. But if you get into a routine of studying while inhaling a pleasing scent, it gives you one more way to maintain your focus and build your study habits. If you are unable to purchase candles or a diffuser, any clean, natural scent is better than a bad one. Just try to keep your space clean—and your dirty socks out of smelling range.

HEARING: HIT PLAY ON THE RIGHT PLAYLIST

Many athletes are motivated by hype music during or before workouts, practice, and competition. It can be the same for you as a scholar. In this case, though, you're not necessarily looking to get hyped up. Instead, you've got to find the pieces that take your brain to a calm zone. It could be classical music, sounds in nature, binary beats, instrumental, or acoustic. Whatever the genre, it should be music you enjoy listening to in the background that won't distract you from reading or writing.

Make a playlist called "Study" out of these tracks ahead of time, so you don't have to cue up a new song after each one ends. This can be done using a paid streaming service like Spotify or Apple Music, or for free using YouTube or Pandora. The idea is to get your mind into a focused, uninterrupted rhythm and create a study-friendly ambience.

You could also get a small desktop fountain to provide the soothing sound of flowing water. You can find relatively inexpensive ones online. I have a tiny pineapple fountain on a back table in my classroom, and several of my students, especially those who have ADHD, request to sit there during independent work time.

TOUCH: FIND SOMETHING TO SQUEEZE OR SOMETHING THAT SQUEEZES YOU

Many people are kinesthetic learners, meaning they learn best when their bodies are in motion. If this sounds like you, you might find that squeezing playdough or a stress ball can help you as you read or write by lowering anxiety, blood pressure, and stress levels.

You might be wondering, what about fidget spinners? I'd advise against them, because a fidget spinner's motion isn't continual. You spin it, hold it between your fingers for a few seconds, and then turn it again. It's more like a fidget enabler and concentration-breaker.

Another idea is to integrate relaxation tools into your learning space. A few personal favorites in my study sanctuary at home are massagers. I have a foot, knee, and hand massager by my desk. In my chair, I also have a back warmer and back massager. Granted, these aren't cheap. So if they aren't an option for you right now, look online for directions on making a rice sock, which is inexpensive, easy, and effective. Or you could try something as simple as placing a warm cloth on the back of your neck or on your forehead. Another option is to try some of the finger tapping meditation techniques from the Tapping Solution app. They can help you relax and focus before studying, during breaks, or while winding down after you finish studying.

TASTE: SIP ON SOMETHING TASTY, CHEW ON SOMETHING CHEWY

A final way to look forward to studying and setting the mood is to treat yourself to a special drink, like hot or iced tea, a favorite beverage from a coffee shop, lemonade, a small soft drink, or a water with a squeezed lemon slice in it. These liquids can enhance, rather than impair, your awareness and enjoyment. If you study late at night, just be sure you aren't drinking anything caffeinated. I don't want you going zombie mode on me the next day.

You could also chew your favorite flavor of gum while studying. Multiple research studies have suggested that with other variables being equal, gum-chewers perform better in answering multiple-choice questions than non-chewers. In one study, gum chewing even increased alertness among students. This last suggestion could be more of a folk tale than fact, but it does seem as though chewing the same flavor of gum (like mint or strawberry) while studying and then while taking a test might improve students' performance. It's possible the brain and memory thrive off an association between the material you've studied and the taste that went along with your study. Anyhow, what harm can it do to try? (Other than possibly annoying the test-taker beside you . . . so just remember to chew with your mouth closed.)

THE MAGIC OF ENVIRONMENT

As you set up your study sanctuary, consider one more example of how powerful your environment can be: In their book *The Power of Moments*, Chip and Dan Heath share a story about a little girl who had just finished receiving a scan from an MRI machine at a hospital. She had to stay very still for nearly 30 minutes in claustrophobic conditions paired with loud mechanical noises.

And yet, when she got out of the scan room, she asked her mom if she could come back to the hospital again the next day to do it again. Why? Because of GE Healthcare's Adventure Series, an innovative program that turns an overwhelming experience into an enjoyable one.

This girl's MRI room had been painted to look like a pirate ship, not a hospital. To reach the MRI machine, she walked a plank. On a side wall, she saw a monkey with a banana. Rather than focusing on a potentially scary brain scan, she felt like she was joining a pirate crew.

What's the lesson here? Part of blazing our trail is reframing our environment. We can keep it bland or make it magical and transformative. We can turn unpleasantness into pleasure. We can turn desks into study sanctuaries, and when we show up with our hearts and minds wide open, we can be rewarded with a sense of inner peace, success, wisdom, and academic enlightenment.

CREATE YOUR HAPPY PLACE

In 2013 and 2016, the same nation was ranked as the happiest in the world. Care to guess which nation I'm talking about?

The answer is Denmark. *Denmark?* Depending on the climate you're used to, you might find that surprising. Denmark's winters bring short days, long nights, temperatures below freezing, and a fair share of rain and snow. It isn't especially easy or comfortable to spend a lot of time outside socializing or exercising during the season. But the geography and climate have presented Danes with an opportunity to make their homes their happy place.

They refer to this as hygge (pronounced HYOO-guh), a Danish word that means "coziness." As Meik Wiking explains in *The Little Book of Hygge*, Danes use fireplaces, cocoa, pastries, a variety of candles, and the frequent company of friends and family to snuggle up and embrace the darkest of seasons. They get the lighting just right, cook tasty treats together, and open their social doors (while their home's physical doors stay closed to keep it warm inside).

So now the question becomes, how can you make your home hygge? Scratch that. How can you make your personal space hygge? Your parents might make you burn this book if you plaster the family room with BTS posters and blame it on me, but you might be able to get away with it in your bedroom. And if you share that room, you can still create a hygge corner all your own.

CRAFT YOUR HYGGE HAVEN

Think of hygge as making your own little universe. Not a galaxy far, far away. A universe you can call home. A universe family and friends can visit and enjoy alongside you. What are some of your favorite things? Your sun and stars? Movies? Sports? Video games? Books? Music? How can your space reflect your unique personality and desires, creating a sense of calm, acceptance, and independence? It's not an escape from the outside world. It's a new world—one you get to design yourself.

Here are a few ideas of what you could put in or around your room:

- Potpourri, incense, or a diffuser with a favorite scent
- LED lights along the walls or ceiling

- Small sculptures, figurines, crystals, or other objects that give you pleasure to look at or hold
- Posters or other visuals of your favorite artworks, or your own works of art
- Posters of musicians you admire
- A way to listen to your favorite music
- Board games, decks of cards, or video games

Maybe as you prepare to make this transformation of your room or other space, you want to draw a blueprint or create a running list of ideas on your phone. But as you think about the things and the ambience that you like, don't forget that there's a second aspect we need to consider: your universe must be welcoming to others. That's a big part of the Danish concept too. The idea isn't that the Danes lock themselves up in isolation all winter. Instead, they create a warm and friendly space where others can join them. So think of ways to make your little universe inviting to the people you hope to share it with. And if you only have a portion of a room because you share your space with someone, try to find some things that bring you both joy.

Lastly, there's one duty you'll have after you build your own hygge. It's an ongoing task. You have to keep it clean! Crumbs and empty pop cans? Not hygge. Pile of dirty clothes pile in a corner? Not hygge. Smells like a locker room? Definitely not hygge!

When I was a teen, my friends and I had our own hygge spaces, even if we didn't call them that. I was obsessed with sports—mostly basketball, football, and baseball—and I also collected sports cards and figures. At a thrift shop, my dad bought me a locker for my room, where I could hang up my jerseys, keep my shoes, and store my best cards and memorabilia. I also had a small indoor basketball and a net that hung on my door. My friends and I would play against each other during sleepovers.

We weren't an affluent family, and maybe you don't come from money, either. If that's the case, remember that thrift shops, eBay, and yard sales can often provide what you're looking for without costing much. So can neighborhood "Buy Nothing" groups, where everything is free!

One of my best friends from high school had dreams of going to film school and working in Hollywood. His family certainly wasn't wealthy, either. But he worked hard to create a space that supported and inspired his dreams. He earned and saved money so he could fill his room with favorite movie posters, shelves of DVDs, a sophisticated camera, a TV with speakers, and a computer to play around with pictures and video clips he'd taken. After high school, he went to film school. And, to this day, he works on sets, helping film and produce TV shows and movies you and your parents have likely seen. His bedroom became his happy place, creating his happy life.

You need to know you are not just decorating a room. You are also expressing and celebrating your whole self. Past you, present you, and, hopefully, future you.

CHAPTER 14

EXPRESS YOUR GRATITUDE TO HONOR YOUR HEROES

BEST TEACHER EVER

In *The How of Happiness*, research psychologist Sonja Lyubomirsky discusses a surprising study about gratitude.

In the experiment, researchers studied three random groups of people for six weeks. During that time, researchers asked the first group to write five things they were grateful for in a journal three days a week. The second group was required to register the same gratitude list, but only once a week. And the third group didn't keep a gratitude journal at all.

One point became apparent from the study, which wasn't too unexpected: participants in group two had become happier because of the gratitude exercise, while the third group didn't. The surprising part? The second group also reported more happiness than the first group! Like the third group, the first group reported no significant change in their level of happiness throughout the experiment.

How can a group who recorded their gratitude only occasionally (once per week) become happier than a group who did it frequently (three times a week)? According to Lyubomirsky, these results could suggest that if you practice gratitude too often, it begins to feel like a monotonous chore that you *have* to do instead of an exciting expression you *get* to do. So it's important to find the sweet spot between not expressing gratitude at all, and feeling genuine, authentic gratitude for our lives.

One more key element? We need to express that gratitude not only to ourselves, but also to others for how they help us. This is a win-win because it boosts our joy while also bringing pleasure to the person receiving our thanks or our gifts.

If you don't feel like you're a naturally grateful, optimistic person, don't worry—you are not at a disadvantage. This is a skill anyone can learn. Plus, there's already a template we can use to help us remember to give thanks: our calendars.

HOLIDAYS WORTH HONORING

There are many days built into our calendars when we can show appreciation for our social network and the ways they help us, large and small.

Think about all the opportunities: Father's Day, Mother's Day, Valentine's Day, Memorial Day, Labor Day, Veterans Day, Teacher Appreciation Day, Siblings Day, Diwali, Thanksgiving, Christmas, Hanukkah, Eid al-Fitr, the new year, wedding anniversaries, birthdays of friends and family . . . the list goes on.

These are annual opportunities to show thankfulness. And remember that making or buying a gift and writing a letter or card are not chores you do because you have to. They're opportunities to strengthen your gratitude muscles.

GENERIC VS. GENUINE GIFTS OF GRATITUDE

This is no time to go generic. When you're expressing authentic gratitude, it's important to stay true to yourself—your brand, if you like—with thoughtful, personalized, and specific cards and gifts.

For example, let's say you're picking out a birthday card for someone you're dating. Are they really into romantic books and movies? Are they very expressive? A poetic card that speaks to your relationship could be the best option. Or, if they are comical and goofy, you could pick out a funny card to make them laugh. The card should show that you've deeply thought about their personality and your current relationship with them.

And you can take the card to the next level by writing a sweet note rather than a basic one. Not just, *"Happy Birthday! I hope all your birthday wishes come true!"* but something more like this:

Hey Bae,

I just wanted to wish you a Happy Birthday. You've helped me so much since we've been together. Remember when I was having a hard time with my parents' divorce and those girls at school, and I called you crying? You stayed on the phone with me for over an hour, listened to me while I cried, and helped cheer me up. I felt so alone when my parents split up and when I lost that friend group, but I also felt hopeful knowing you loved me and were there for me. I keep thinking about our favorite scene in Stranger Things *and how it's like our story. When I feel like Vecna is coming for me, I hear your voice, almost like Lucas, "I'm right here." And just like Max, I'll keep running up that hill to you. I hope you enjoy the movie tickets so you can go with a friend or me soon.*

Love,

———————

See the differences between the first and second messages? Anyone can write the first, but the second takes a genuine heart, introspection, and description. What specifically do you love and appreciate about your friends or family members? What have they done for you over time? What memories have you made together that speak to your larger story? What do you want to do with them in the future? You can answer these questions in a card that will make you grateful for each other.

Or what about a gift for a holiday like Mother's Day? Googling "Mother's Day gifts" is a decent starting point, but what is *your* mom into? Does she have a favorite sports team, hobby, or author? Would she like concert tickets or yardwork supplies? Books or music or clothes or home decor? You might need to figure out a clever way to get some intel. You could subtly ask some questions about what she's loving right now. You could pay close attention to what she looks at in shops or talks about at the dinner table, and jot down three or four ideas on your phone. You could even talk to another family member or friend and get their thoughts before making a decision. What she might most enjoy, though, could be spending some quality time with you, like watching a show or cooking a meal together.

THE MONUMENTS ALONG YOUR PATH

When you take time to honor a hero in your life, it is like creating a monument of that person on your unique path—and also on theirs. It's expressing gratitude for someone who has helped you, supported you, or even made sacrifices for you. Someone who has inspired you to continue on your path of purpose.

Monuments honor others, and they also remind you that you're not alone as you blaze your trail.

CHAPTER 15

END WITH GRATITUDE

Complaining.

We all do it, some more than others, and, in some cases, rightfully so. Life can be crappy sometimes, and complaining is a natural response to BS.

Let's say you get a terrible haircut. You drop your cell phone and crack the screen. The person you're dating cheats on you. You get a flat tire or have car trouble. A close friend becomes a distant stranger. You get blamed and grounded for something you didn't even do.

Each of these situations is frustrating or discouraging in its own way. And when they happen, we tend to complain, let it ruin our mood, and even define our day. It's natural—but there's a better way.

A SHIFTING TECHNIQUE

Jon Gordon is a motivational speaker and writer. In his book *The No Complaining Rule*, he offers a strategy for transitioning from complaining about everyday challenges and frustrations to accepting them—and even being grateful for some of the obstacles we face. It's called the "but" technique (the conjunction, not the body part). It's simple . . . *but* effective. When you complain, don't end that sentence with a period. Instead, add a "but" and try to end with a positive thought.

- *I don't love this haircut, but at least I have hair. It'll grow back.*
- *I hate that my phone is cracked, but I'm grateful I can still call my friends and family.*
- *I'm hurt that they cheated on me, but now that I know I can't trust them, I can find someone who deserves my affection.*
- *It stinks that I got a flat tire, but I know I'm lucky to have a car.*
- *I'm disappointed the friendship fell through, but it can motivate me to try and make some new friends.*
- *I'm mad about being grounded when I know I did nothing wrong, but I'll have a lot of time on my hands, so now's my chance to do some research on college scholarships.*

Sometimes, a simple conjunction and a few encouraging words can shift your whole outlook. Now, I'm not talking about the deep traumas in life, such as poverty, abuse, neglect, racism, the death of a loved one, or a natural disaster. Talking about these experiences isn't complaining. It's processing and, hopefully, moving toward healing. But for the smaller-scale challenges that crop up in your path, give this technique a try. It might prove to be more powerful than you expect.

THE THREE OPTIONS

In *The Happiness Advantage*, Shawn Achor outlines three possible ways a situation can go when you're faced with adversity:

1. The adverse event produces no change, so the result is neither positive nor negative. There is no movement.

2. The adverse event creates more negativity in your life, resulting in negative consequences overall. You move backward.

3. The adverse event leads to a positive change, and the overall result is positive. You move forward.

When a challenge hits, you can't control the initial event—the bad haircut, cracked phone, unfaithful partner, flat tire, alienated friend, or punishment from your parents. But what you *can* control is your response. Will you stay stagnant because of the challenge, will you move backward, or will you find a glimmer of good in the bad and move forward? Choose the third option. I'm not suggesting that you can't complain. I'm saying, don't end with the complaint. Research supports the idea of gratitude journaling to increase your sense of happiness. You could, for example, list the bad thing that happened and four good things that could result from that bad thing in a notebook or diary.

AMOR FATI

Amor fati means taking this whole gratitude concept to the next level. It means "lover of fate." Essentially, you embrace whatever life throws at you as destiny, and you grow to love and value it eventually, even if you hate it initially.

The ancient Stoics embodied this idea skillfully, especially Marcus Aurelius. During his reign as emperor of Rome, he faced countless obstacles, and met them with grit and hope. Early in his power, a pandemic called the Antonine Plague spread through the country, killing an estimated five million people or more. Several of his own children even died under his reign. There was also a significant famine in the land. The nation was in debt, and its people lacked food and water. His army was fighting a war that would last five years. Rome was collapsing, yet it seems that Marcus Aurelius answered each challenge with amor fati—with a *but*. Perhaps he told himself messages like these:

- *Our people are sick and dying, but I can offer them some small comfort and bring us all together by giving inspirational speeches and attending funerals.*

- *Our nation and citizens are in debt, but I can sell the empire's treasures to raise money for the people.*

- *Our soldiers are being attacked, but I can leave my palace for the front lines to lead them and fight alongside them.*

I had an awakening of amor fati myself while writing this chapter. As I wrote, I was battling a tough situation. When I was a kid, my dad and I had a pretty difficult relationship. I was wild and unruly, and he was somewhat stern—not an easy mix. We weren't compatible when I was growing up.

Then I graduated from high school and went on to college. As I said in chapter 12, I almost failed out after my first semester. I went back home to face my dad, expecting, at the very least, a verbal spanking. Instead, he handed me a book. He told me he loved me and thought it was a significant time for me to read it. It was a novel called *The Traveler's Gift* by Andy Andrews, about a man going through a hard time and lacking a vision for his future.

He crashes his car and, in a dream state, travels back in time to receive life lessons from seven famous figures, including Harry Truman, Anne Frank, King Solomon, and Joshua Chamberlain. They teach him values and lessons about things such as owning your mistakes, seeking wisdom, and persisting without exception. The man eventually wakes up, puts these lessons into practice, and goes on to lead a joy-filled, meaningful life.

The following semester, I changed my minor to history, took extra classes, and graduated on time with a 3.5 GPA. I've been teaching history ever since.

In the years after my dad gave me that book, both of our hearts softened. He was there beside me every step moving forward. He was the best man at my wedding and seated beside me as I waited for my kids' births. When I was in rehab for depression, anxiety, and a prescription drug dependency and no one else would come to visit me, he drove over an hour each day to see me for a week straight. He helped me paint my classroom Carolina blue once I started teaching, and he brought our entire family stacks of gifts each Christmas. He'd show up for both grandkids' sports games to cheer them on. For the last few years, he'd been bringing us dinner every Thursday night. We would eat, play board games, and watch the Charlotte Hornets or *Ted Lasso* together on TV. Since college, my dad has been a cheerleader for the rest of my family and me. It's been healing and refreshing.

That's just part of why it was so hard when I got a call from a nurse at a nearby hospital that my dad was experiencing congestive heart failure and was unresponsive. I ran out my front door, jumped into my car, and sped to the hospital like a NASCAR driver, sobbing and gasping for air as I wove through traffic. I knew in my spirit that my dad was dying, so I didn't ask a higher power for him to be saved. I simply prayed he could hold on long enough for me to be with him one last time. After parking and running up to his room, I faced a brutal scene. Several doctors and nurses were huddled around my dad, doing chest compressions.

I could see him from the hallway, but hospital personnel were guarding the door and wouldn't let me in. I felt helpless. All I could think to do was what my dad had done for me for so many years—be a cheerleader. I started clapping from the hallway and screaming to him so he could hear my voice, "Hold on, Dad. I'm right here. Come back to me. I'm here. I'm not going anywhere. Stay with me, Dad. You can do this."

Shortly after that moment, he regained his pulse. He came back for me. The doctors started preparing to move him to the ICU, but things quickly took a turn for the worse. A doctor let me into the room and said he only had a few minutes left. I sat beside my father, held his hand, and told him how legendary of a father and grandfather he was, how incredibly blessed I was to be his son, and that he could let go when he was ready to be at peace. I put my head on his shoulder and felt his cold hand squeeze mine as he took his final breaths.

Then, the words from a nurse, "Time of death—7:32 p.m."

The machines turned off. The doctors left, and the door closed. The room was silent. Just my dad's body and me.

I haven't been able to get it all out of my head. For weeks, my dad's death haunted me, but researching and writing this chapter helped me include gratitude even in sentences that flow with grief.

- *My dad died, but I'm grateful we didn't give up on each other after a rough start.*
- *My dad died, but I'm thankful he returned to me so I could be with him one last time and say goodbye.*

- *My dad died, but I'm going to love, serve, and give like he did to keep his legacy alive.*

Amor fati, lover of fate. It's finding *something* to love and embrace in even the worst situation. I don't love that my dad died, but if his story had to end at that moment, I love that I was able to get there in time to be with him. I love that he waited for me. I love what he taught me over the years, and I will add it as fuel to the fire that will burn for the rest of my life as a teacher, husband, father, and if I'm lucky, grandfather.

How can you work a *but* into whatever you are going through right now? Maybe you're dealing with a lack of acceptance or interest from a friend group or a guy or girl you are into. Maybe you didn't get accepted to your first-choice college and can't decide which college you want to attend—or you *did* get accepted but don't know how you'll pay for it. Maybe something is happening at home that scares or worries you. Maybe a doctor told you unsettling news about your physical or mental health. No matter what the situation, can you find a glimmer of hope or brightness in it—however small?

Remember what Marcus Aurelius said: "A blazing fire makes flame and brightness out of everything that is thrown into it."

Not just the good things—*everything*. So let's take what life gives us and make a blazing fire. Let's use our adversities as warmth for our souls and light for our paths. We can do this.

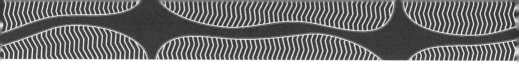

PART THREE

THE ONWARD PATH

GO NOMAD

Jared Grano was in ninth grade when his dad, a middle school principal, decided the whole family would be taking a vacation to Walnut Canyon National Monument, near Flagstaff, Arizona.

Initially, Jared admits, he wasn't expecting anything interesting. That began to change as he walked through the canyon trails with his family and learned about the Sinagua people, who had lived there almost 900 years ago. He saw animals like elk and javelina, and he noticed the bushes and pine trees.

And then the canyon suddenly grew dark. As rain and sleet began to fall, the family retreated into a cave. Jared heard thunder echo through the canyon and saw flashes of lightning. He looked out from the cave into the rain and, in his words, "finally felt that I was a part of nature."

NATURE HEALS

Jared's experience is shared in Richard Louv's bestselling book *Last Child in the Woods*, where he describes nature-deficit disorder as a condition that many modern people experience because they aren't connected to the natural world around them, suffering from side effects like:

- diminished use of senses
- inability to concentrate
- increased rate of physical and emotional illness

Louv argues that connections with nature like the one Jared experienced can help young people who are struggling. And science supports this theory. In a research study discussed in Stephen Ilardi's book *The Depression Cure*, an anthropologist interviewed members of the Kaluli people, who live in Papua New Guinea and forage, grow crops, and hunt. The researcher was looking for signs of clinical depression. Out of over 2,000 adults and children, only one person seemed to approach the criteria for a diagnosis.

None of them had a cell phone. No Netflix, no TikTok. No cars and no cash. And virtually no signs of clinical depression. I don't deny that there is a chemical component to depression. Still, this study and others strongly suggest that a person's environment also plays a big role. And one lesson I took from *The Depression Cure* is the importance of movement and nature.

The Kaluli people are constantly in nature—exploring the rainforest, walking trails, and gathering food for their communities. I'm willing to bet that this positively affects their physical and emotional well-being.

You probably can't just decide to pick up and move to the rainforest. But we can all get outdoors from time to time, move our bodies, and reconnect with nature—no matter where we live. So go nomad. Head to the woods, mountains, or beach—or just to a park or other outside space. Move. Explore. You're not hunting for animals in the wilderness. You're hunting for peace of mind, to slow down the wheels of time, and, like Jared, "be a part of nature."

THE NOMAD PLAN

Make a list of paths, trails, greenways, parks, and other outdoor places you can visit. It's great if some of these can be natural areas away from a big city, but the important thing is to put some distance—even a little bit—between yourself and home or school, and move your body while out in nature. Try to get out to one of these places once a week, if you can. Sometimes, ask family members if they'll join you, and other days, see if a few friends would be interested. Occasionally, if you feel comfortable and safe, walk alone. Here are six tips to get you started:

1. Make a list of 20 greenways, nature trails, paths, or hikes in your area. Depending on where you live and what kind of transportation you have, look for places you can get to by bus or train or in a short amount of time.

2. If you like, download the free Under Armour apps MapMyWalk or MapMyRide, where you can set goals and challenge yourself for walking, jogging, or biking.

3. Set a weekly, monthly, or yearly goal, and try to challenge yourself. You could focus on your pace of walking or biking, the distance you go, or the time you spend.

4. Pack a bag with anything you'll need for your outing—water, snacks, sunscreen, bug spray, sunglasses, gloves, and so on.

5. Reach out to a few family members and friends to see who would be interested in going nomad with you.

6. Set aside one day on the weekend or each week to walk or bike, maybe at a local trail during the week, or one that's farther away if you take a weekend outing.

As I said, I strongly believe this will improve your mind. And it can also strengthen your body. That doesn't mean you have to make this a strenuous workout. But just about every type of movement you do stretches your tendons, uses your muscles, and engages your heart and lungs. Going nomad can be a physical and emotional retreat—and also an advance into greater well-being and health.

MOVEMENT AND STILLNESS

If you go to the woods and observe nature, you'll notice a rhythm of movement and stillness. That's how we are meant to be, too—not busy all the time or none of it, but instead enjoying a balance of working, playing, and resting. Movement and stillness intertwined.

Squirrels leap from tree to tree, playing tag. Birds sing with one another on a branch. Turtles sunbathe on a log. A deer gazes off into the unknown. A breeze bends the trees. Leaves fall in slow motion, cradled back and forth by the wind until they are laid to rest on a gentle river, going wherever the current of destiny leads them.

This is the rhythm of the woods, something we've long forgotten. Before our busy schedules, we used to be one with nature, but then came television, video games, skyscrapers, cars, cramped classrooms, computer screens, and social media. No wonder many of us feel lost or depressed—we've forgotten a part of who we are. But with a simple walk in the woods, you can begin to remember.

REDISCOVER CHILDHOOD HOBBIES

Let's take a quick trip back to your elementary school days.

You've been watching the clock, waiting for recess to begin. You can't wait to go outside, feel the sun on your face, and spend time with your friends on the playground or the sports field.

Or maybe you were counting down the minutes to your "specials" or elective class, like art, music, dance, orchestra, or band.

What was your go-to game at recess? Was it 4-square, kickball, tag, or hide and seek? When you got home, what did you enjoy playing with your friends in the neighborhood? Was it Capture the Flag, riding bikes or scooters, or basketball?

What about your favorite specials activity? Was it drawing a self-portrait or painting abstract art? Did you lose your sense of time playing the trumpet or clarinet? Did you really find your voice and build a connection with others through performing in a musical?

All these games and hobbies probably shared one truth: you enjoyed them because they were a good time, pure and simple. There was no pressure to win. Instead, the focus was on the love of the game, performing, and forming bonds with friends. Your role in these activities was not to be the most elite player, best painter, or first chair, but to be part of something—for fun, for friendship, or just for the hell of it.

Fast forward to today. Have you recently tried out for a school team? Did you get cut? Was someone chosen over you for a big part? Did you see a peer's artwork and think, "I could never draw like that." If so, you're not alone. I know that feeling as well. It's more than disappointment. It's a feeling of "I'm not good enough." For many of us, it can make us want to quit the activity altogether. We forget about the experiences we had in the past that made it enjoyable and worth it. Now it's all about the final score or a fancy ribbon. The championship. The starring role. The MVP award. The recognition. There is a clear shift in focus. The hobby becomes a battle or competition, focused on a singular outcome and stealing the joy of the process. It takes the place of quality time with your friends, and you suddenly see them more as competitors than companions.

Or let's say you *did* make the team or get the lead role. Congrats! But I bet you feel the weight of pressure on your shoulders too. Will you start in the next game? Or will you ride the bench more often than not and still end up feeling disappointed, frustrated, or not good enough? Will you receive a standing ovation, or will you forget your lines and embarrass yourself in front of the crowd? Maybe you start comparing yourself to your fellow players, even though you're all on the same team. It's a dangerous game when, rather than running your own race, you focus on someone else's.

THE COMPARISON TRAP

Mitch Prinstein, a psychologist at the University of North Carolina, points out in a *Psychology Today* article, "When we're reliant on others for our sense of self, only feeling good if we get positive feedback or markers of status, we're at risk for depression."

This is the "comparison trap." You might not have fallen into it very often in elementary school, but these days you may feel like you get caught in it a lot. As you've gotten older, your brain has developed more processing power. You're more aware of others' abilities as well as your own—and how they might be similar or different. But this kind of awareness can be a weakness or a strength. To make sure it gives you focus, encouragement, and energy—rather than dragging you down or making you feel crummy about yourself—try to use the knowledge you've gained and turn that tension into positive action. Are you going to quit, or hustle more? Are you going to let not making the eighth-grade soccer team define the rest of your athletic experience? Will you define your artistry as a whole because one piece of your art wasn't well received?

I think it's time to develop a new mindset about athletics and the arts. Think about why you participated in the first place. Do you have a childhood hero who inspired you? Maybe you aspire to be the next Serena Williams, Lionel Messi, Millie Bobby Brown, or Taylor Swift. Perhaps you had a fantastic coach or teacher who praised your talent. Or you wanted to be a part of a team or band with your friends. Maybe the desire to belong to an elite group that turns into a close-knit family is your "why." But then your name didn't make that list, you didn't join the cast of a play, you weren't chosen to be a member of the band, you didn't make the team, or you lost an art competition.

Here's the new perspective I propose: The main purpose of playing and creating doesn't have to be beating someone else, securing a trophy, getting a scholarship, or gaining anyone's approval. It's not only about winning. It is about movement and self-expression. It's about collaborating with others. You can create a bond that doesn't break when you lose. You can become the best version of yourself in this new light.

Here are a couple of questions to ask yourself. Their answers could help you transition into that new mindset of not participating in a hobby to win, make a lot of money, or become famous, but because it's an important value—an ingrained element in your life.

- When I've participated in physical activities or the arts in the past, how did it positively impact my mind, body, and social life? Did I feel happier afterward? Did I sleep better that night? Even though my muscles were sore for a few days, did I eventually become faster and stronger if I kept at it? Did I build connections with other players on my team and maybe even my competitors?

- What opportunities are available in my area right now for low-key athletics or artistic expression? Pick-up basketball or soccer games in the neighborhood or at a nearby park? A cricket club team at the YMCA? An intramural sport at a high school or college campus? A free gardening, cooking, pottery, or carpentry class at the community center or online? How will I make a plan to give one of these a try?

CONNECTION > COMPETITION

What about if you aren't on a team or connected with other creators (yet)? Your passion doesn't have to end here. You can still reignite your desire to get off the bench and work toward being a champion. Think about this: A group of researchers from UC Berkeley tracked the correlation between interaction and success within NBA teams. They did so in an unusual way—by counting the number of high fives or fist bumps given during games at the beginning of the season.

By the end of the season, they discovered that the teams who had given more high fives and fist bumps also had more wins and played with more cohesion. By constantly lifting each other with a simple act of physical touch, these teams were better able to shake off the bad plays, boost their mood, and keep pushing. By hearkening back to playing like kids on the blacktop—offering gestures of praise or encouragement—they became champions.

Clearly, team activities can be about connection and collaboration as much as competition. So if you don't make the school team, look for other opportunities to engage—maybe playing on a team at the YMCA, YWCA, or a local recreational league. You could also join Big Brothers Big Sisters of America, a mentoring program that serves thousands of kids and teens, including those in military families or with parents who are incarcerated. This program carefully matches up kids and teens with successful adult mentors. And there's a Sports Buddies program within Big Brothers Big Sisters focused specifically on watching and playing sports, where mentors coach, counsel, and participate in games and events with their mentees.

POSITIVE TRANSFER

You could also try a new sport or art form. Maybe you're not the next Serena or Messi because you are supposed to be the first you. The skills you're developing now can help you improve at other activities. This is called positive transfer. For example, if you've learned to do an overhand volleyball serve, this can positively transfer to serving in a tennis match. If you can use your fingers to play a song on the guitar, you might also be inclined to find your rhythm on a pottery wheel. When you can transfer your knowledge and skills this way, it's like you have a head start. It will help you naturally feel successful in something new to you because of your previous success in something old.

Another positive transfer would be coaching kids in a sport or hobby you've always been passionate about. You can use this knowledge for the rest of your life. Your passion may or may not have made you the best performer, but as a coach or mentor, it can give you the potential to help someone else strive for greatness and build deeper meaning and purpose.

THE LASSO WAY

Ted Lasso, the fictional coach on the hit show of the same name, is not a typical coach in the world of European soccer (also called football). Before he is hired to coach the AFC Richmond soccer team in England, he had only coached US football. But what he lacks in soccer experience, he makes up with his energy, his kindness, and his love for growth.

Lasso gifts an older player, Roy, with the book *A Wrinkle in Time* to help him realize he is the team's leader as well as one within his family. When Sam, a rookie, is playing defense during practice, an opponent causes him to fall, and Sam is embarrassed and frustrated. Lasso encourages him by asking, "You know what the happiest animal on Earth is? It's a goldfish. You know why? It's got a ten-second memory." He even calls Jamie, the self-absorbed superstar of the team, into his office, where he calmly counsels him, "I think that you might be so sure that you're one in a million, that sometimes you forget that out there you're just one of eleven." And to all his players, Lasso explains that the ultimate goal of playing is not about winning and losing, but about being the best version of yourself—on and off the field. Sports can become a blueprint for the game of life.

Try to harness this sort of energy and positivity when you're facing a challenge. It's not easy, but next time you miss a goal, lose a game, or are cut from a team, try not to see it as a competition you've lost. Instead, try to embrace it as an opportunity to become a better version of yourself, to play for a deeper purpose.

Once Lasso gets his players to buy into the ideas that soccer should be fun and that it should be a chance to embrace their inner child, something surprising happens—they start winning. It's almost like they went back in time, counting down the seconds until recess when they could run onto the field to play with their friends and feel the sun on their faces.

CHAPTER 18

EAT A FROG OR MAKE
A SNOWBALL

Do you have so many assignments, projects, and tests to complete that you don't even know where to start?

Even outside of school, do you worry about how you will complete these tasks? Do you have anxiety about the grades you'll earn?

And are you nervous about how you'll fulfill your after-school obligations, like chores, a job, volunteering, or music, dance, or sports practice?

If your answer is yes to any of these questions, there's bad and good news. The bad news is that these thoughts alone can derail you, push you to procrastinate, and limit your academic performance. The good news? You can tackle this with a notebook, a pack of sticky notes, and a pen or pencil. You can turn the anxiety into action.

Here's what you'll do:

1. **SET UP YOUR TASK NOTEBOOK.** When you're in class at school, any time a teacher tells you about an assignment, project, or test that you will need to do or prepare for outside of class, write it down on the first blank page of your notebook. If they give you a due date, record that date beside the name of the task.

2. **SET UP YOUR DAILY TASK LIST.** Each morning before school begins, whether you're at home, on the bus, or in homeroom, open your Task Notebook and look at what's coming up. Then pull a sticky note from your sticky note pack and record the tasks you will do for the day. *But,* you might be wondering, *how should I organize the tasks?* That's a great question. Here are two options:

   a. **Eat a Frog:** Mark Twain, one of the great authors and humorists in US history, once said, "If it's your job to eat a frog, it's best to do it first thing in the morning. And if it's your job to eat two frogs, it's best to eat the biggest one first." Twain wasn't talking about eating that poor amphibian you recently dissected in biology class. Instead, as Brian Tracy has pointed out in his book, *Eat That Frog!*, what Twain meant was that when you have multiple tasks to complete in a day, it can help to "begin with the biggest, hardest, and most important task first." Why? Well, for one thing, think about how good you'll feel once it's done. You'll have a sense of pride and accomplishment. You ate a freaking frog first thing in the morning. Go you!

The Eat a Frog method of organizing your task list is all about prioritizing and organizing in difficulty from most complex to easiest. So if this is the approach you choose, write the tasks in a numbered list on the sticky note, with the first being the most difficult and the last being the easiest to complete. You start with the frog, and work your way toward the stuff that's a bit easier to swallow.

b. **Make a Snowball:** As someone with ADHD, this second method works better for me. The snowball strategy is pretty much the reverse of the frog method. Imagine waking up one morning and looking out your window to see the ground covered in a beautiful, thick blanket of snow. You throw your clothes on and run outside to build a giant snowball. Maybe you'll throw it at your brother, or maybe it'll be the beginning of a snowman. Either way, what do you do? Most likely, you'll start with a small handful of snow, shape it into a ball, set it on the ground, and then slowly roll it or pack it with the surrounding snow until it's as big as a boulder.

This is how I make my days productive. At some point in every school year, I end up with so many tasks in my notebook that they take up multiple pages. It's hard to figure out where to start. So, I pick the most manageable tasks and write those on a sticky note first. Then I gradually record the ones that are more difficult until I end the day with the giant snowball. That way, I'm slowly taking consistent action throughout the day and making consistent progress. Toward the end of the day, I have built up enough positive momentum to finish creating my snowball—even if I'm feeling cold or tired—because I know how close I am to the finish line, and how far I've come.

3. **CROSS THE TASKS OFF THE LIST.** As you finish each assignment or project, cross it off your list. This process releases endorphins in your brain, a hormone that makes you feel happier.

Now that you've documented your assignments, created a new task-completion system, and put your plan on paper, thoughts about the work don't have to swirl around your mind so much. If the worry or stress do start to rise, you can gently remind yourself, "I have a plan for that. I'll get it done," and bring yourself back to the present moment.

So each day, eat a frog or make a snowball. It might not always be quite that easy—but it *is* that simple.

CHAPTER 19

SKETCH OUT A WEEKEND PLAN

Picture yourself standing in front of a classroom full of your peers and teacher. It's your turn to give a project presentation, but you've got nothing prepared. No slideshow or other visuals. No critical points on index cards to talk about. No speech to read from. *Nothing.* How do you think that presentation would go?

You might fumble around with your words, trying to speak about a topic you haven't researched. There would likely be plenty of awkward silences. Other students might begin doodling on papers—or putting their heads on their desks in despair. Every second that passed would feel like an hour, and it would be wasted time for everyone because there was nothing to teach, learn, or experience.

THE PROBLEM WITH FREESTYLE WEEKENDS

You would never do a presentation without a plan, so why would you go into each weekend without one?

Don't get me wrong—I understand. I can see how the last thing you might want to do when you leave school on Friday is follow a weekend plan, especially after feeling like most of the school week has been planned out by the adults in your lives. Maybe you feel burnt out by the week's grind and go home craving sleep like a bear in the winter. You may feel like it's time to hibernate—barricading yourself in your room, sleeping late, taking naps in the afternoon, maybe watching TV or reading or playing video games.

It seems logical: work all week, rest all weekend. But there's a problem with this theory. After a weekend of doing nothing, do you feel more gratification or less on Sunday night when you look back at your time spent? Do you feel more or less tired on Monday morning when you go to school?

In his audiobook *Midlife and the Great Unknown: Finding Courage and Clarity Through Poetry*, poet David Whyte shared a conversation he had with an Austrian friend—a Catholic monk named David. During an incredibly tiring season in Whyte's life, he said to his friend, "Speak to me about exhaustion."

Brother David's response was enlightening: "You know, the antidote to exhaustion isn't necessarily rest. The antidote to exhaustion is wholeheartedness."

After you spill some combination of blood, sweat, and tears at school, part of your weekend certainly should be spent at rest. But a lot of it should also be spent awake and feeling truly alive—living with a whole heart. If you're with me here, let's make that our aim: *wholehearted weekends*.

Now, I'm not suggesting that you get to spend every moment of the weekend at play, either—wholehearted or otherwise. Your laundry pile could grow as big as Mount Everest in just a few weeks. Chores and tidying up need attention too. The trick is to categorize and maximize your time with enjoyable, meaningful, productive, and active tasks. And to do that effectively, you'll need a plan.

I'll show you how to sketch a weekend plan. As a model, I'm using a template similar to what I'd use to create a lesson plan in my classroom. And it will only take you a few minutes to complete each Friday night or Saturday morning. It doesn't need to be thorough, just organized. Here's what it could look like in a journal, on a sheet of paper, or sticky note.

Objective

Start with an objective, setting the intention for what's to follow. Here's an example of two weekend goals I might put at the top of the page (you can use my goals or create your own):

1. Enjoy the weekend.

2. Recharge for the school week.

Schedule

Next, flesh out what needs to happen. When doing this, mix together your must-do's and your get-to-do's. Must-do's are chores, such as loading the dishwasher. And get-to-do's are fun, such as going to the movies with a friend.

My son Cole's schedule might look like this:

Time	Activity
Friday Night	sleepover with Gavin and Landon
Saturday Morning	wash, dry, and fold laundry
Saturday Afternoon	play basketball with neighborhood friends
Saturday Evening	watch movie with fam
Sunday Morning	read and write comic books
Sunday Afternoon	play Nintendo Switch and Oculus
Sunday Evening	go on a nature walk with fam

It's likely that your must-do and get-to-do lists will vary each weekend. One weekend, your parents might make you mow the lawn, and it takes up half the day, but during the following weekend, you somehow squeeze in a workout, manicure, and pedicure all before lunch on Saturday. The focus here is not hitting a specific number of things to do, or achieving the same ratio of rest, fun, and chores every time. Instead, the idea is to habitually maximize your weekend time after working all week. During the school week, you had to follow schedules created by others. But now, you have some power to make your own schedule!

Assessment

The final part of a teacher's lesson plan is assessment. That's how we evaluate whether the activities we are doing in class are working. To make sure your weekend plan is working, test yourself with a three-question assessment each Monday morning:

1. How do I feel when I look back on my weekend?
2. What do I think about the week ahead?
3. Was my weekend with a plan more fulfilling than past weekends without one?

If your answers are positive, your plan is working!

It can also help to look at the bigger picture after a few months. If you begin to notice you're overwhelmed with things you must do on the weekends, stop and analyze each part of your schedule. What can you say no to? What can you cut out? Is every must-do *truly* a must?

ONE LAST THING: DON'T FORGET TO DIFFERENTIATE!

You probably already know that not everyone learns exactly the same way. (And you can learn more about this in chapter 20.) Some students learn faster than others, some enjoy working in groups, and others prefer independent learning. One person might learn a lot about the anatomy of a frog by reading a chapter in a science book, another by watching a video about a frog, and another by dissecting a frog. One might even learn by eating a frog. (Wait—scratch that. Don't literally eat a frog! I'm getting my chapters mixed up.)

That's why good teachers try to present topics in multiple ways to suit each student's needs, reach every type of learner, and enrich the experience for everyone. It's a form of differentiation that personalizes the experience for each learner. The best weekend planners use this same strategy, incorporating a variety of different kinds of get-to-do's. For instance:

- **Social versus solitary:** The weekend is a great time to be with friends and family. Be sure to connect with others, but also make time to withdraw—time when you can meditate, read, journal, color, or write by yourself. Just you. Even if it's only for a few minutes each weekend, make time to be a hermit as well as a social butterfly. Bounce back and forth from one to the other.

- **Outdoor versus indoor:** The simple act of exposing your skin to sun and fresh air can provide a little spark of happiness. Try to do at least one thing outside every Saturday or Sunday, whether it's a jog, a bike ride, a kayaking adventure—or just a meal with a friend at a picnic table or on a patio. Other activities in your plan, from gaming and reading to homework and chores, will provide plenty of time indoors, so work on being intentional about getting outdoors when the weather allows.

- **Physical versus mental:** Physical exercise has tons of benefits. When you curl dumbbells, run on a treadmill, or play a sport, you're caring for your body, releasing endorphins in your brain, and stepping up your energy level for the days ahead. But just hitting the gym isn't enough. It's equally important to give your brain a workout. Try cooking a new recipe. Do a crossword puzzle. Play chess, checkers, Monopoly, or another game. Join a book club. Listen to a TED Talk, take a MasterClass, or do one of The Great Courses. Go back and forth between stretching your mind and body all weekend long.

Weekends aren't just about rest. They are also about rejuvenation. So make a plan to get the most out of your days off, and then put that plan on your phone, a calendar, or an index card. That way you won't snooze through the weekend. You'll enjoy it, learn from it, grow because of it—and most of all, you'll experience it wholeheartedly.

CHAPTER 20

BREAK FREE FROM SELF-DOUBT

Have you ever seen a video of a trained elephant? Have you ever wondered how trainers can lead an adult elephant around with just a single, small rope? These are some of the world's largest and most powerful animals, after all. Why don't they break free?

BABY ELEPHANTS AND LEARNED HELPLESSNESS

In his audiobook *Accelerated Learning Techniques,* motivational speaker Brian Tracy explains how this is done. Trainers capture baby elephants and use ropes to tether them to poles. The baby elephants try to break loose and return to the wild, but eventually give up after repeatedly failing. Even when one of these animals grows into adulthood and reaches its peak physical power, the elephant believes in its mind that the tiny rope is more powerful—keeping it trapped. This is called learned helplessness, the false belief that we can't do something in the present because we couldn't do it in the past.

I'm curious if something like this has ever happened to you. Maybe a coach cut you from a team because you weren't athletic enough at the time. Or perhaps a teacher wrote something negative about your behavior or academic performance in a report card, in an email to your parent, or in red ink on an essay paper. Maybe you were rejected by a crush. Or another student might have posted something on social media or a text thread that made you feel ugly, weird, or stupid. And you took it all to heart. That criticism didn't just trap you for a moment—it's still trapping you now. You've accepted it as a part of your identity, even though you are stronger, smarter, and more talented than you were in the past. But you can move on. You can break free.

EXPLORING MULTIPLE INTELLIGENCES

I believe that one thing trapping a lot of us is the idea that some people are smart and others are dumb. Which is, quite possibly, the dumbest idea I've ever heard. The truth is, we are all intelligent—just not in exactly the same ways. Some people are smart with numbers, others with art, some with sports, and others with nature. Every one of these facets of intelligence requires brain activity, and scientists have found that people who are smart in a particular area have a higher brain function in a specific part of the brain related to that measure.

You can break free from self-doubt, beginning with a mindset shift revealed in Carol Dweck's best-selling book *Mindset: The New Psychology of Success*. It's all about moving from what she calls a fixed mindset to a growth mindset.

Someone with a fixed mindset might think, "I've never been able to break free from this, and I never will. I'm stuck for good. Why even try?" But a pachyderm with a growth mindset would see it differently: "I can't break this rope . . . *yet*. But I'm going to keep trying. I know I can get stronger, tougher, and smarter, and eventually, I will break free." It can take time to develop a growth mindset, but it's powerful. It reminds you that failure is part of learning, and that just because you don't have a certain skill yet, that doesn't mean you can't build or strengthen your ability.

So don't let anyone in this world make you feel stupid. Every supposed weakness comes with a strength. Every curse comes with a blessing. Each of us is already intelligent in some ways, and you have opportunities to become smarter in other areas if you are confident and willing to put in the work. When we know and accept that truth, the knowledge can help us escape past criticism, failures, and self-doubt—rather than allowing a letter grade, teacher, parent, or system to define us and keep us bound by that tiny rope. We can roam free and step into a genuine, limitless future. The trick is to know our own intellectual gifts, use them to increase our self-confidence, create conditions for growth, and maybe even pick another area or two of interest that we can develop over time.

So, what are these types of intelligence? Howard Gardner, a psychologist from Harvard University, came up with a theory of multiple intelligences, hypothesizing that there are many different ways to be wise, not just in school but in life. He also proposed that we each have some level of intelligence in all these areas but are stronger in some than in others. Here are the various intelligences he identified—plus one of my own.

1. **BODY SMARTS (BODILY-KINESTHETIC INTELLIGENCE):** If your favorite part of the school day is recess or physical education—or if you can spend hours running, biking, playing a sport, doing gymnastics, dancing, or playing board games without getting bored—you might be sports smart. I can point out my body smarts students within a few minutes of sitting in class, because they are the ones who can't sit still. Their bodies crave movement, whether they're learning, playing, or working. And when they have the opportunity to move or work with their hands and feet, they often feel better and learn better.

2. **MUSIC SMARTS (MUSICAL INTELLIGENCE):** With this intelligence, it's all about loving the rhythm. The right song can transform your vibe and get you singing, humming, or dancing along. You may like to play an instrument, attend concerts, play *Beat Saber* or *Guitar Hero*, or even make your own beats or lyrics. Your favorite classes could include music, dance, band, or orchestra. Music smart people are usually in touch with their feelings and use music to connect, embrace, and healthily express those emotions.

3. **LIFE SMARTS (EXISTENTIAL INTELLIGENCE):** Life smart people are the philosophers and the spiritual ones. They enjoy meditating deeply on the big questions like the meaning of life and the possibilities of the afterlife. Many can point back to moments of profound, transcendent experiences, even in childhood. They are fascinated by culture and religion—both their own and those of others around the globe. Some may feel most at home in a place of worship or some other spot that feels deeply meaningful to them. They are in tune,

not necessarily with music, but with the rhythm of the heavens and the universe.

4. **PEOPLE SMARTS (INTERPERSONAL INTELLIGENCE):** The people smart teens like to sit at the mall or on a park bench and observe the people around them. They like examining others' behavior, enjoy being around many people, and have a robust social network. At a party, they're the magnets everyone gravitates to. They are good at connecting with others by telling stories, asking the right questions, and giving compliments in conversations. They are also typically empaths—able to feel the emotions of others, in part by picking up on body language or reading between the lines of a person's words or actions.

5. **ART SMARTS (SPATIAL INTELLIGENCE):** If you sometimes get into trouble in class for doodling on your paper or drawing on Procreate using your iPad, you're probably art smart. Or perhaps you see clothes and shoes as ways to express yourself through fashion. Art smart people love posting videos on social media or taking pictures for the school yearbook or paper—or simply for their own pleasure. They may enjoy taking in paintings at art museums or creating artwork of their own. Being art smart is having a love for what only images can express.

6. **NATURE SMARTS (NATURALIST INTELLIGENCE):** Nature smart teens feel most at peace on trails through the woods, playing at the beach, or listening to the waterfalls in the mountains. They love animals—petting them, holding them, playing with them, feeding them, and even scooping up their poop (well, maybe not that last one). Some nature smart people are also fascinated by crystals and the healing potential they might hold. Their favorite class is usually a science where they can study plants, animals, rocks, and minerals. And their favorite field trips? Aquariums, zoos, and nature museums.

7. **WORD SMARTS (LINGUISTIC INTELLIGENCE):** If you're word smart, you likely enjoy reading and writing, playing word games like Scrabble and Wordle, and sharing jokes or hearing puns. At school, you're probably going to be all about language arts classes, checking out books at the media center, and participating in debates during social studies. Word smart people are typically strong communicators with others but also highly value time alone to interact with language, almost like it's a good friend.

8. **LOGIC SMARTS (LOGICAL-MATHEMATICAL INTELLIGENCE):** Logic smart teens are fascinated by numbers, like sports statistics or stock fluctuations. They take great pleasure in playing competitive board games as well as puzzle-solving video and online games. As students, they usually do best in classes related to subjects like math, science, and statistics.

9. **SELF-SMARTS (INTRAPERSONAL INTELLIGENCE):** Self-smart people have high emotional intelligence. They are reflective and very much in tune with their own feelings, values, and goals. They tend to have a clear understanding of why they do what they do, and feel what they feel. And they are usually able to motivate themselves, rather than relying on others. If a teacher were to ask them who they would like to work with for a group project, their answer might be "Myself!" They value time alone over time with others, journaling over writing a text message, and silence over the din of a crowd. They know that when they spend time with themselves, they are in good company.

10. **TECH SMARTS (TECHNOLOGICAL INTELLIGENCE):** Gardner doesn't include this intelligence in his theory, but I believe it deserves to be on the list. Tech smart teens can easily navigate every Snapchat filter, create a funny TikTok video mix, or stream their gameplay with exciting commentary on Twitch. They may love coding, building

websites, or even assembling computers. They enjoy communicating with, and learning through, technology. These are the future digital creators, fixers, and influencers.

After reading about these kinds of intelligence, what new questions or ideas do you have? Has anything shifted in the way you perceive yourself—and what you see as your potential or your limitations? Are you interested in learning more about these ideas, like ways to become more competent in a domain or where an intelligence could lead you in a future career? And are you simply wondering how to know where *your* strongest intelligence lies?

When it comes to that last question, you can find a tool to help determine your top two intelligences by searching online for "literacynet.org" and "find your strengths." The site contains a free, quick survey that, once completed, will provide fun ways for you to put your top two areas of smarts to good use. To learn even more, I also highly recommend *You're Smarter Than You Think*, a book by Thomas Armstrong, which delves deeper into multiple intelligences. It's informative, intriguing, and empowering.

Above all, I hope you'll use these ideas and this information to reclaim your own power and break away from whatever past experiences might be holding you back. Remember those elephants from the beginning of this chapter? Consider this: In the wild, elephants are a keystone species, shaping their entire habitat so other animals can thrive. For instance, some elephants use their tusks to dig up dry riverbeds, creating water holes where thirsty animals can drink. They can weigh up to seven tons, and, depending on their species, can live for as long as 70 years with their herd. And yet, when they're taught to be helpless—to believe they are weaker and less magnificent than they truly are—they can be held captive.

Before reading this chapter, maybe you sometimes felt helpless or worthless. You may have thought you had little to offer this world. Maybe you looked around at other students, teammates, or siblings and felt inferior. Maybe you often whispered to yourself, "I'm so stupid."

If any of this is true, it's time for a new voice to take hold. Not a whisper, but a powerful affirmation: "I am body smart!" Or "I am art smart!" Or how about "I am people smart!" Whatever your intelligences are, repeat them to yourself. Visualize yourself breaking the ropes that have held you. You were born to find your power and purpose, to use your authentic gifts, to help the people and the world around you in ways only you can, and to enjoy and exercise your strengths.

CHAPTER 21

SPEAK AND WRITE FROM THE HEAD AND THE HEART

What does it mean to speak and write from the head and heart?

To speak from the head is to communicate like a scholar—in a way that's thoughtful and civil. And to write from the heart is to enlighten others with empathy, humility, and grace; to care more about how your message could help others than how it might help you.

This chapter explores a range of tools to help you connect with others through speaking and writing, whether you're taking part in a class or club debate, talking with a family member or friends about touchy topics, writing a blog post, composing an essay, or even authoring a book. Some ideas come from modern ideas like the behaviors of civil discourse and advice from poets like Amanda Gorman. Others, like Tonglen, are drawn from ancient Buddhist philosophy.

The following ideas may be easy to read but can be quite difficult to put into practice. Nevertheless, I encourage you to try. I'm certain you'll find them to be rewarding ways to build bridges rather than walls.

SPEAKING: ADOPTING THE BEHAVIORS OF CIVIL DISCOURSE

I imagine you have strong opinions about plenty of things. In fact, we all have unique perspectives that deserve to be heard, no matter where they fall politically, spiritually, or culturally. And it's natural that, when we express those perspectives, others will sometimes disagree with us. Differences of opinion are part of life, and part of society. But they don't have to be cause for conflict. As long as we aren't saying anything hateful, it can be incredibly valuable to engage in passionate yet respectful conversations with people who hold opposing viewpoints.

The bad news is that—as you may have noticed—a lot of the adults in my generation haven't exactly set the best example for this. Social media is filled with finger-pointing, name-calling, and aggressive language. In person, friends or family members may get into vehement and even aggressive arguments. At their worst, these arguments can lead to people feeling like they're engaging in battle rather than conversation, seeking to destroy the enemy with their words.

The *good* news is that if you find yourself in a disagreement with others in a class, out with friends, or at home, there are some tried-and-true ways to do better than my peers and I have. You can have more intellectual, productive, and respectful discussions. One framework I like comes from the website Edutopia, which lists six behaviors of civil discourse. Here are the two my students have found most helpful in our class conversations:

- **"Challenge ideas, not individuals."** The essential idea here is to never attack the person making the point you disagree with, but instead to focus on disputing the argument they're making. To do this, try listening and responding with sentence starters such as, "I hear where you are coming from, but my perspective is that…" or "What I'm hearing is…" or "I see what you're saying, but what I'm thinking is…." This comes across as a lot more rational and academic than yelling, interrupting, or name-calling. And it can help everyone involved remember that there are real people—with real feelings—on the other side of the conversation.

- **"Commit to learning, not winning."** Try treating the interaction as more of a discussion than a debate. In that context, you aren't necessarily trying to convince the other person you're right. You're not expecting that everyone in the room will come to a universal conclusion or agreement about a political, religious, or philosophical stance. Instead, everyone is listening to and learning from each other. You are each getting an opportunity to see the world through a different lens. In the end, you may know more about the other person and even about yourself.

These guidelines may seem simple, but they can make a big difference. As a young person, you have an important voice. You can give the world a unique perspective on the problems previous generations have created or left unsolved, like social injustices, climate change, poverty, and hunger. You might even have innovative ideas for solving them using new technologies or strategies. And yet, if you aren't able to communicate your ideas in a kind, confident, and diplomatic way, others tend to shut down and get defensive—including the people who most need to hear your message.

WRITING: DON'T DO IT FOR THE FAME

Let me share a story I heard about a young girl who fell in love with writing when she was seven.

Because she had a speech impediment and an auditory processing disorder, communicating through spoken language could be hard for her. But writing opened up a whole new way of expressing herself. So she poured her heart into writing, as well as reading. Over time, she learned more and more about the art of writing, like how to recognize and use rhetorical devices such as metaphor (connecting two things that might seem very different), simile (comparing one thing to another using *like* or *as*), personification (giving humanlike characteristics to an animal or object), alliteration (making similar sounds flow together), and anaphora (repeating the same word or phrase at the beginning of each sentence or line).

By 2021, this young girl had become a young woman—and a poet. She beautifully performed her energizing poem "The Hill We Climb"at the presidential inauguration of Joe Biden. She was only 22, the youngest inaugural poet in US history. Her name is Amanda Gorman.

After her recitation, Gorman became famous, but I love what she said in her MasterClass about why and how she writes: "The reason I do what I do isn't fame. It isn't attention. It's to make a difference, and if I can remind myself of that purpose every single time I pick up the pen, then the heat and intensity of the spotlight is really rendered insignificant because it's more so me wanting to use the spotlight on issues that matter."

What about you? Why do you write? Do you do it only when it's an assignment? Or do you enjoy writing stories, poems, or songs on your own time? Maybe you're an avid letter writer or blogger. In any case, I propose an idea: When you write, whether it's for school, for your own pleasure, or for some other purpose, consider Amanda's words and try to tap into your natural empathy. Think about how your writing can make a difference and connect you to other people. Remember that even though your journey is your own, it can and does affect others—for better or for worse. Which means that sometimes, blazing your path is about listening to, speaking with, and writing for or about people around you—people who are on their own trails. It's about seeing the emotions behind others' experiences. Listening, penning, connecting, sharing, and inspiring on issues that matter.

One way of building empathy that I really like is a practice that Tibetan Buddhists call Tonglen. It's a literal and figurative meditation technique for breathing in the world's suffering (including your own) and breathing out loving-kindness to yourself and all who are suffering. It can help you feel more deeply tied to the world and all its people, ease your own pain, and empathize with the pain of others—including people you don't especially like, or might not even know. That's what Amanda Gorman did when she wrote "The Hill We Climb," and when she shared it with a people and a nation who had suffered greatly.

BE HUMBLE. SIT DOWN.

So, let's say you've worked hard at speaking and writing like a scholar. You've practiced and improved. Eventually, you might even begin to feel like a natural, an expert among the crowd. You might . . . dare I say . . . start feeling a little cocky. If that's the case, please let me offer an anecdote from my personal history.

Several years ago, I began doing public speaking by training other teachers. I would primarily teach them about making learning engaging for students, along with how they could maintain a work/life balance that was healthy and sustainable for them.

When I first started, my lectures were mediocre at best. After a while, I started figuring out how to engage the audience better. I asked them questions, moved around the room instead of standing in one space, replaced my nervous *umms* and *aahs* with short silent breaths, performed a rap I wrote to teach my students about the Bill of Rights, and shared personal stories like my recovery from depression and addiction.

After speaking for a few years, I had an event in my hometown, Charlotte, North Carolina. There was a huge turnout. I was talking to several hundred teachers, and I felt comfortable being so close to home. I hit my stride from the moment I took the mic. The jokes landed, and the teachers clapped along to the rap. As I finished, they were leaning toward me in their chairs—and then the crowd jumped to their feet, hootin' and hollerin' with applause. It was my first standing ovation! I strutted back to my seat as if I'd just won the Super Bowl.

When I sat down in my chair, the director of the event slipped me a little note. I thought it might say something like, "That was amazing!"

Instead, it read, "Zip up your pants."

I share this embarrassing story to illustrate an important point: There are *always* opportunities to do better and to grow. Even when Marcus Aurelius was in his final years as emperor of Rome—one of the most powerful people in the ancient world—he still read stacks of books and visited a teacher so he could learn and grow. I think iconic rapper Kendrick Lamar summed it up best in his song "Humble." "Be humble. Sit down." Speaking and writing from the head and the heart—from the brain and the spirit—requires a commitment to being a lifelong learner, and that means staying humble. It means never entirely buying into the idea that you've become some kind of celebrity, genius, or all-knowing king . . . *especially* if your pants are unzipped.

CHAPTER 22

HOLD THE CONVERSATION WITH ANXIETY

While being a trailblazer can be a solitary pursuit at times, I have a feeling there might be one companion who will visit you periodically on your trek.

You might be making significant progress, feeling the sun on your face and the breeze in your hair, hearing the birds sing in their chorus among the trees, and then, bam! Out of nowhere, this individual will walk up beside you and start asking you questions.

They mean well. They are not trying to hurt you. In fact, they are trying to *protect* you from being damaged. Even so, if you let them talk too much, they can get your heart racing, your blood pumping, and your mind spinning. What's their name? Anxiety.

When Anxiety shows up on your trail, it's best treated not as an enemy but simply as a friend who desires a conversation. It can slow you down or even derail you as it works to convince you to take a "safer" path. But if you are equipped and willing to hold your own in that conversation, you can continue moving forward.

WHAT DOES ANXIETY SOUND LIKE?

Anxiety loves to ask questions. Questions like:

- *What if you can't fall asleep until 2 a.m. again tonight?*
- *What if you fail math for the quarter and your dad takes your cell phone?*
- *What if you're discriminated against because of racism?*
- *What if you ask someone out and they say no?*
- *What if you come out to your friends and they don't accept you?*
- *What if you have a terrible game and let your team down?*
- *What if you forget your lines in front of the whole audience?*
- *What if you do something stupid and disappoint your family?*
- *What if you go to the party and no one wants to talk to you?*

COGNITIVE DISTORTIONS

If you meditate on Anxiety's questions too often or for too long, or if you do so emotionally and not logically, they can create what psychiatrist and researcher Aaron Beck described as *cognitive distortions*, or negative thinking patterns. These thoughts can loop in your brain like a song on repeat. They can distort your reality and trick you into thinking things that are often false and destructive.

Here are several types of cognitive distortions as outlined by Beck and one of his students, David Burns:

All-or-Nothing Thinking	Perceiving situations, the world, and yourself only in extreme terms, leaving no room for gray areas or nuance
Blaming Others	Placing the responsibility for a situation entirely on others, without taking some of the ownership yourself
Catastrophizing	Believing the worst possible scenario will happen in the future, even without evidence to support that expectation
Emotional Reasoning	Accepting that something is true solely based on a feeling you have about it, rather than on objective facts or logic
Fortune Telling	Making pessimistic predictions about what's going to happen next with little or no evidence to back them up

Labeling	Making a negative judgment about a thing, person, or entire group of people with little evidence
Magnifying the Negative and Minimizing the Positive	Zooming in on negative thoughts and losing the more extensive picture, while reducing the volume or importance of anything good
Mind Reading	Pretending to know what others are thinking; making assumptions about how they feel
Overgeneralization	Having one bad experience and believing that experience will repeat itself in every future situation
Self-Blaming	Taking all the responsibility for a failure, even for factors outside your sphere of influence
"Should" Statements	Making rigid rules about how you and others should behave, setting unrealistic expectations

HOLDING THE CONVERSATION

The good news is that you can respond to the cognitive distortions Anxiety uses by *reframing* the concerns more rationally and holding that conversation with Anxiety in a peaceful, positive manner.

This is the basic idea of Cognitive Behavioral Therapy (CBT). You can learn about reframing by working with a counselor specializing in CBT, using the techniques in this chapter, or—my personal favorite—using a CBT workbook or anti-anxiety notebook. (You can find many of these online.)

CBT builds your resilience so that you don't feel so bothered by these interactions with Anxiety. Let's try this out and respond to a few of those questions Anxiety might ask:

ANXIETY: "What if you can't fall asleep until 2 a.m. again tonight?"

TRAILBLAZER: "Aren't you overgeneralizing a little here? It was one bad night. Since I'm so tired from last night, tonight could be my rebound sleep. I'll stay active today, and I bet I'll be so exhausted by the time I get in bed that nothing can keep me from falling asleep and getting the rest I need. Even if that's not true, I survived today on a few hours, and I'll survive tomorrow too."

ANXIETY: "What if you fail math for the quarter and your dad takes your cell phone?"

TRAILBLAZER: "Easy there, Chicken Little. The sky isn't falling. The world will not end if I don't have my cell phone, and it certainly won't end if I fail math. My dad would likely be disappointed, and I would be too. But I will focus on what I can do now to improve my performance instead of catastrophizing and worrying about what could happen later. Here's my plan: I'm going to ask Dad to help me find a tutor, email my teacher for extra support and extra credit, watch a few videos on Khan Academy, and sit away from my friends and in the front of the classroom to minimize distractions during each lesson. I think that's a pretty reasonable plan."

ANXIETY: "What if you're discriminated against because of racism?"

TRAILBLAZER: "I know there are racist people out there. But there are also anti-racists. So I'm not going to label everyone as discriminatory or prejudiced. What I will do is show courage and search for inclusive people.

I will buy their products and eat at their restaurants when I find them. I'll support them as they support me. And I'll spend my time and energy with friends or family with me who love and respect me for who I am."

ANXIETY: "What if you ask someone out and they say no?"
TRAILBLAZER: "Have you been staring into a crystal ball? Are you asking a tarot card reader about my love life? Are you a fortune teller? The way I see it, they can respond in one of three ways: 'Yes,' 'No,' or 'Not right now, but maybe later.' So I've got a two-thirds chance of them not flat-out turning me down, and I'll take those odds over yours any day."

If Anxiety wants to walk with you, there will be times when you just have to let that happen. But don't let it talk as long as it wants. And when Anxiety bombards you with those annoying questions, talk back. Don't let it be a one-way conversation. Remind yourself of the cognitive distortions that might be at work. Step back, take a moment, and then use your *own* voice to take control and find serenity and clarity.

PRACTICE THE ART OF KINTSUGI

What is depression?

I can't know for sure if it's the same for everyone, but the depression I've seen in others, and the depression I've felt in my own spirit, can be summarized in one word: brokenness.

With depression, things you used to enjoy doing no longer bring you joy. It feels like your smiling muscles are broken. You carry the shame of a past mistake or are angry about a trauma you experienced when you were younger. It feels like your heart is broken. A family member or friend dies and you'd give almost anything to hear their voice or see their face once more. It feels like your soul is shattered. You see no purpose to life, nor feel any hope for your future. With all the suffering that surely lies ahead, what's the point? Your give-a-shit meter is broken.

There was a time when you felt complete, but like a bowl that smashed onto the floor, depression broke you into a hundred little pieces.

Depression is a natural human experience for many. And it doesn't care if you're powerful, or rich, or admired, or successful. It can affect anyone. As historian Joshua Wolf Shenk explores in *Lincoln's Melancholy*, even Abraham Lincoln had depression. (In the 1800s, it was referred to as *melancholy*.) The Civil War–era hero is widely considered the most significant US president. He held the Union together and helped Black Americans earn their freedom. He also experienced a great deal of suffering. For example, he profoundly grieved the loss of his mother when he was nine. Later in life, two of Lincoln's sons died as children, leaving him debilitated with sadness. He sometimes spent entire days in bed, experienced nightmares about his death, and had suicidal thoughts that kept him from carrying a knife out of fear he might harm himself with it.

> If you find yourself having suicidal thoughts or making a plan to harm yourself, I urge you to put this book down and talk to a therapist, school counselor, parent, or teacher you trust. Or call or text 988 to reach the Suicide & Crisis Lifeline. You are not alone, and there is help.

Depression can happen for a day, or for a season, or, like Lincoln, it may be with us for a lifetime. I'm not here to tell you we can eliminate or control this mental state. But I believe that—like Lincoln—we can still lead meaningful, helpful lives with sparks of joy and leadership. To do so, we need to build skills for caring for ourselves and coping with the negative energy in our minds.

UNSKILLFUL VS. SKILLFUL

If you have had depression before—that confusing and all-consuming sense of hopelessness regardless of reality—I could argue that, even if it seems counterintuitive, that experience gave you an advantage: you survived it.

The longer you have had depression, and the more you reflect on it, the better you can become at working with it as an energy. The skillful are the enlightened ones, the awakened ones. They accept sadness as a part of their experience, but not something that completely defines them. It may be part of your life, but it is not *all* of your life—even if it feels that way at times. And I truly believe this is something that can inspire you to hope. Mental illness may make life seem hazy and unclear, but by using strategic thinking patterns, you can move forward. Depression is like a fog that can cause you to stumble on a dark night, but hope is the lantern you can carry. It illuminates the path when you can only see a few inches in front of your face.

The following ideas can help you move from unskillful to skillful ways of working with depression, moving from hopelessness to peace.

SELF-HARM VS. SELF-LOVE

"What if I want to cut myself?"

Have you cut yourself before?

Maybe you were being bullied at school and felt like you couldn't take it another day. Or perhaps you felt a huge amount of pressure from your parents and were afraid you'd let them down. Maybe you looked in the mirror and didn't like the person looking back at you. You hated yourself, so you self-harmed. You thought it would somehow release the negative emotions you had about yourself. It's not that you wanted to end your life—but you *did* want to express your suffering.

Over time, though, this way of coping will not really help you feel better. So, to help you find other strategies to deal with difficult feelings and emotions, I want you to prepare to have an honest conversation with yourself. Next time you consider cutting, here are five questions you can ask yourself:

1. What negative thoughts are filling my mind right now?

2. Where did I get the idea of cutting as a strategy for coping with suffering?

3. In the long run, how effective or healthy is cutting as a way to cope with suffering?

4. What is a healthier way I can cope with suffering?

5. Who can I talk to when I'm struggling with these feelings and thoughts?

These questions can lead you to *self-love* and *self-care*. They can help you interrupt the cycle of negative thoughts that might lead you to harm yourself and give you a moment to make a new and healthier plan to care for yourself. You can play a sport, practice positive self-talk, create art, watch a movie with friends, watch a comedy show, talk to an adult you trust, or take a walk. These are ways you can truly heal—not by adding physical scars to emotional wounds, but by *closing* emotional wounds before they create physical scars.

BINGE-WATCHING VS. BINGE-WALKING

"What if I want to be alone and binge-watch shows all day?"

Do you ever get the desire to retreat to your bedroom, close the door, and watch a whole season of a favorite TV show? Well, I have a piece of news: That's normal for people with depression.

Isolation is a strategy—a cruel trick of the mind. It can make us think, "The outside world hurts me so much I just want to close it out. Maybe I'll be happy on my own private island." In small doses, this can be helpful. Sometimes we need time alone to relax after a stressful day of school, process a loss or breakup, and escape our real-life stories by immersing ourselves in ones on TV.

But an entire day? Or multiple days? That's when the solution becomes more of a problem. That's when you can become secluded and stuck. So instead, what if you mix it up, and alternate between isolation and inter-action? Try watching 30 minutes of a movie or one episode—and then hit pause. Next, mix stillness with movement, even if that movement is going to another room to have a simple exchange with a family member or friend. Talk to them about your show, the things that intrigue you about the char-acters, and exciting plot twists. Engage with others in a way that helps you open up to make new connections.

You can also try taking this a step further by getting outside and moving for 30 minutes. Walk around your neighborhood or nature trails with a family member, or talk with a friend on the phone while you walk. Play a sport with others or go for a bike ride with someone. Then, if you still want to, you can go back to the TV for another 30 minutes and repeat the process all over again. See if this rhythm is more helpful than continual isolation.

AWFUL VS. UNPREFERABLE

"What if my life sucks and I hate everything?"

When I ask teens why they are depressed, these are the two most common responses: My life sucks, and I hate everything.

Of course, that doesn't actually tell me much about what's really going on for them. So I dig for more information, and find out that they mean something like this:

- I hate getting out of bed and getting up early for school.
- I hate one of my classes because the other students are so loud.
- I hate hearing my parents fight.
- I hate doing my homework.
- I hate getting lectures from my parents about what I should do when they don't even take their own advice.
- I hate how I look.
- I hate how little time I have to hang out with my friends at school.
- I hate being punished for my classmates' mistakes when I did nothing wrong.
- I hate my brother because he's so annoying.

It may be a cliché to say this, but *hate* is a really strong word—a loaded word. There's so much wrapped up in it. What if we switch the word *hate* with the phrase *don't prefer* to take the emotional intensity out of it?

"I *don't prefer* my third block class." "I *don't prefer* getting out of bed early." "I *don't prefer* how I look today."

There's a big difference between *hated* and *not preferred*. Or between awful and unpreferable (which isn't technically a word, but I *prefer* to make it one for this chapter!). And while it might seem like a small or even superficial change, when we can switch the words we use in our heads, it can make a big difference for the better. On the flip side, when we allow our most negative thoughts and comments about situations to echo in our minds, it can make life seem much worse than it is.

And, if we're being honest, does our entire life *really* suck? Or are there simply some things that happen each day that we don't prefer? Most experiences each day are like a ball on a pendulum that swings back and forth between what we do and don't prefer. We can call this the Preference Pendulum.

We can take comfort in knowing that after one class that's loud, the next class is with a more mellow group of students led by a teacher who takes steps to minimize distractions and disruption. We can take comfort in knowing that after we knock out a homework assignment, we can lie in bed and play some video games or listen to music. And I can almost guarantee that you have a higher tolerance for unpleasant tasks and situations than you think. Try to view them as an opportunity to build resilience and patience. And remind yourself that the pendulum is swinging toward the unpreferable right now, but it will swing back toward what you prefer soon enough.

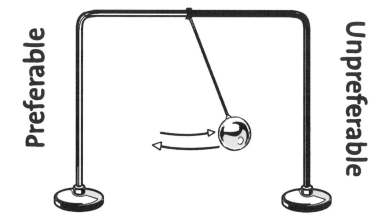

Another strategy is to use logic to play a little joke on your emotional brain. My counselor used this technique with me after I lamented about a day we had on our family trip to Disney World. We were pumped to go on a brand-new ride, but the FastPasses we purchased to skip the line didn't work and we had to wait in line for over three hours. Then, halfway through the ride, it shut off. We had to unbuckle our seats and walk to the exit without experiencing the full ride— just as the park was about to close for the night. I was disappointed and miserable.

My counselor's advice was to use my knowledge of history to add some satirical humor to the situation by saying to myself, "If you thought it was terrible for the US soldiers in World War II who stormed the beaches of Normandy against machine-gun fire, let me tell you about the time I waited an entire day at Disney World with my family to ride a ride until . . . gasp, it broke down halfway through!"

At first, my face turned red, and I was slightly offended. Then, we both laughed hysterically. He was right. The satire of this exaggeration helped my rational brain get my emotional mind in check. Still, I didn't find it pleasant at first. It felt a bit like emotional suppression. And yet, when I started using this strategy daily, I was surprised at how quickly I became a happier and more grateful human.

What about situations that are not only unpreferable but genuinely awful? What if I have a family member who dies? What if I'm terribly injured in an accident? What if I'm wrongly convicted of a crime and have to spend time in prison?

When the truly awful takes you into deeper darkness on your trail, look for the lighthouses—the people who have found meaning and crafted purpose out of challenging or tragic situations.

You could follow a lighthouse like Candy Lightner. She lost her 13-year-old daughter, Cari, because of a drunk driver in 1980. In response, she created Mothers Against Drunk Driving, a nationwide organization that has brought awareness to this issue and probably saved countless lives.

You could also follow a lighthouse like Nick Vujicic, an Australian-American who was born with significant physical challenges. Because of a rare disorder, he has no limbs. He also surfs, raises a family, speaks to fans around the world, and writes books that have made it to the *New York Times* Best Seller List.

Or you could follow a lighthouse like Isaac Wright Jr., a Black man who was wrongfully convicted and sentenced to life in prison. He spent seven years in jail learning about the law, appealing his case, proving his innocence, and eventually earning back the freedom stolen from him. Not only that, but he helped 20 other inmates who were innocent get released early and exonerated.

These lighthouse stories are shining examples of how to walk with courage and strength toward the beacon of light.

HAVE-TO-DO LIST VS. GET-TO-DO LIST

"What if I'm overwhelmed with a long to-do list?"

I'm a list-maker myself, and I know this feeling. When the list gets too long, it can feel impossible to do anything at all.

I try to start each morning by putting all the tasks I need to complete on a sticky note. But when I was teaching during the early part of the pandemic, my list could no longer fit on one sticky note. It was taking two or three!

My counselor suggested I add things I enjoy doing to my list as rewards and integrate enjoyment into each day. So right under "Grade papers," you might see "Play *Resident Evil 4* on the Oculus." Or maybe you'd spot "Watch

Charlotte Hornets game" after "Staff Meeting." This is like making a peanut butter and jelly sandwich. Integrate the sticky with the sweet, the have-to-do's with the get-to-do's. What do you have to do? What do you get to do?

ALCOHOL VS. GREEN TEA

"What if I want to drink something to take the edge off and feel a little better?"

You can use liquids to try and numb the depression. Or you can use them to hydrate, create a sense of calm, and see more clearly.

When you're feeling terrible, beer, liquor, or wine may seem to help initially. But give it a few hours. You feel just as bad, if not worse—so you drink more. If this goes on, over time, your body builds up a tolerance until you can't function without alcohol. This is a dead-end road, so if you are using alcohol or drugs, take a U-turn now while you still can.

It may not sound as fun, but I hope you'll give tea a try. Especially if you experience seasonal depression in the darker and colder winter months, think about how much a warm cup of green tea or herbal tea could help mellow you out. And the best part? There are no adverse side effects, short-term or long-term. No cirrhosis of the liver. No risk of dependency. No hangover. No impairment while driving. Just a warm feeling, without all the consequences.

THE KINTSUGI GUY

Kevin Breel didn't have it easy growing up.

He lived with an alcoholic father. Right after middle school, his best friend died in a car accident. In high school, he was bullied. By his senior year, the onslaught of depression caught up to him.

Alone in his bedroom on a dark February day in Victoria, British Columbia, Kevin wrote a suicide note and prepared to swallow an entire bottle of pills. Before he could, he felt an overwhelming, convicting sense that there was more to him than his depression. It was one part of him, but not all of him. He decided to save himself. He realized his suicide note didn't have to be his final note.

He eventually opened up about his struggle to his mom, who connected him with a counselor. He poured his heart out to that counselor. Through therapy with the counselor, he was able to discover his self-worth and recover. In *Boy Meets Depression*, a book he wrote to help teens who are suffering from the same mental illness, he highlights his revelation:

"I thought relief would come in the form of finding people who accepted me. I never knew that the most important thing was breaking down the high walls of self-hatred and actually accepting myself."

Kevin also went on to share his story in a viral TED Talk called, "Why We Need to Talk About Depression." I highly recommend it. He is wise beyond his years and seems like he has a lot of pages left to write. Kevin showed how a teen could come out of a period of depression even more beautiful and wholehearted than they were before they were depressed . . . before they were broken.

The Japanese have a term for this. Do you know what they do with broken pottery? They don't throw the pieces in a trash can. They gather each piece up and glue them back together using a golden lacquer or golden luster. Pottery that might once have been a nondescript color now shines with streaks of gold. This process is called the art of the kintsugi.

It's a healing middle and beautiful ending to a broken beginning. This is what Lincoln did. This is what Kevin did. This is what you can do. No matter what you face in life, I believe you can discover your streaks of gold, your kintsugi.

CONCLUSION

Throughout this book, we've explored your unique path.

It may look different than the ones your friends are taking. It's important to know this journey isn't always easy. It will be complicated sometimes, and it may take some time to work through those challenges. But I have confidence in you as you continue moving forward.

Let me tell you one more story as we come to a close.

THE RISING SUN

Earlier in the book, I mentioned I went to rehab, but I never told you exactly why.

After teaching for several years, I reached my career's pinnacle. The History Channel named me the North Carolina History Teacher of the Year. My class was on the news for projects we did. My students received high marks on their final tests, and I received praise from my students, their parents, and the principal. By any outside standard, I appeared successful—but I was miserable. I'd lost my way trying to live up to what others expected, and now I found myself in a dark wood.

I was working up to 60 hours a week, sometimes staying up until two or three in the morning and only getting a few hours of sleep. I was entirely dependent on high doses of several medications—Adderall for focus, Xanax for anxiety, and Ambien for sleep. I wasn't spending quality time with my family. My wife had contacted a divorce lawyer. And I only had 100 dollars in my bank account. So what does a lonely, dead-broke, burned-out, pill-popping Teacher of the Year do? He checks into rehab. At that moment, a part of me felt like the sun was setting on my life. The darkness had closed in, and I felt lost and alone.

I didn't want to die by suicide, but I knew I couldn't continue down the path I was on. It was either face death, or face my demons—and perform a course correction. I chose the latter. I stayed in the rehab facility for several days, receiving excellent care from nurses, doctors, and therapists. I participated in individual and group therapy. And I began detoxing from those medications that no longer served my mental health.

Even when I got out of rehab, my life felt like a fog for a while. I just couldn't seem to envision a new path ahead of me. But later that summer, something magical happened. My daughter, Savannah, was born. And she came to this world on an interesting day—July 7th. Or 7/7.

In Las Vegas, 7 is the lucky number. In some spiritual texts, it's a divine number of perfection. And how many days are there in a week? You got it. So I took my daughter's birth date as a stroke of good fortune, a gift from God, and a new week . . . a new *day* in my life. A rising sun. It was the end of the old path, where my whole life revolved around teaching, and the beginning of one focused on values in every dimension of my life. When I held my daughter for the first time, I could finally see that new path clearly.

My days have been brighter ever since. I created a vision board and personal creed that I now live by. I joined a boxing gym and fought my way back to health. I sought counseling independently and also with my wife. We fell back in love and are happily married to this today. I play basketball with my son and board games with my daughter. And I returned to the classroom, where I set healthy boundaries for myself and no longer need pills to cope. I love my students and teaching US history.

Most importantly, I'm living a life true to my purpose. I'm my authentic self—at home, at school, out with friends, and in the boxing gym. Husband, Dad, Mr. Ashley, Justin—he's all the same guy now. I didn't know it when I walked into rehab, but the sun was setting on my old life, only to rise with a new one. And the journey I've taken is why I know you can find that dawn too.

IS YOUR SUN SETTING OR RISING?

Maybe there are times when you feel like your sun is setting.

Perhaps your parents are getting divorced. You might be struggling academically. Maybe you're being bullied, or you didn't make the team. You lost a job. Someone close to you died. You're having a hard time making friends, or you're going through a breakup. You find yourself wondering, *Is this really it for me?*

From someone who's been there, please remember: After every dark night, there's a bright day. At every dead end lies an opportunity to blaze your own trail. The sun rises after it sets, and a new path can start where another ends.

If you have the courage to keep moving forward with a new purpose, your struggle so far in life doesn't just serve as an ending, but propels you to the beginning of something brighter, better, and more meaningful than you could have ever imagined before.

MEMENTO VITAE

Your journey may take some time to work through. But please take note that a big part of my growth came when I realized I didn't have to do it alone. You don't have to, either.

Also, remember that you don't have to strive for perfection on your journey—and you also don't need to rush. Instead, take the time to thoughtfully create and walk your own path.

This time of your life can be an internal reckoning about who you are and who you're becoming, a struggle for identity. Some adults make assumptions and think you've got it easy as a teen, especially if many of your needs are provided for. On the other hand, you may not have as much independence as you prefer, even as you are developing the cognition, impulses, and instincts of an adult. You've got mounting pressures at school, perhaps worrying that your performance there will alter the course of your life. You might believe that there's no room for error as you consider what to do after high school. You may be tempted by drugs or alcohol. You're navigating changing friendships and romantic relationships. These are obstacles you will face, but they are worth climbing over and busting through.

I've learned from many spiritual teachers and philosophers that blazing your own trail is a lifelong pursuit. Trailblazing is something you strive to do until the day you die, until your last breath. There is no finish line. The goal is the journey, and the destination is the path.

When you get to the end of your life and reflect back, there will be immense joy in seeing your unique path etched into the world. You'll be able to see where it intersected with others. You'll see the bridges you built over winding rivers. You can view the cemeteries where you buried the demons who tried to bury you. You can see the glimmer of the monuments you built to honor the heroes of your journey. You can look back on the camps where you rested and the waterfalls that brought tears to your eyes. You will recognize the tragedies and victories you experienced along every step of the way.

Some say your entire life flashes before your eyes just before death, but for pioneers like us, I believe it will be our paths that we see illuminated just before the sun sets. When we reach the end, memento mori will no longer be necessary. We won't have to remember that we will die. Instead, we'll experience memento vitae. We'll know that we have truly lived, and we'll be able to able to reflect on and remember the lives we led.

And you don't have to wait until the end of your journey. One of the great rewards of creating your route is the ability to stop and reflect on your progress along the way.

While this may bring you happiness, happiness is not the ultimate goal. There's a concept even more powerful. Remember, your true north is something more profound—your values. For Stoics, these are called the Cardinal Virtues: courage, justice, temperance, and wisdom. For Buddhists, the goal is the bodhisattva—the awakened heart. For Christians, it's the fruits of the Spirit.

Some examples of values and purpose include loving-kindness, service, leadership, innovation, resilience, adventure, entrepreneurship, gratitude, and fortitude. What about you? What are your values? You can't always choose happiness, but you *can* always choose to live a life guided by the values you hold closest to your heart and mind. And the integrity with which you pursue your purpose serves as a compass, guiding you along the path you're carving—both during these often-challenging teen years, and beyond. It will give you a clear vision of the horizon for the rest of your life.

Wherever you are on your journey, now is the time to get ready and get going. You open your backpack and see you have all the tools necessary to start blazing your trail. You are equipped with your vision board, Teen Squad list, family and friend field trip planner, personal creed, dragon potions, and much more. You can do this. You've got this.

Your sun is rising.

ACKNOWLEDGMENTS

Writing a book and getting it into the hands of readers is a mission that can't be achieved on your own. It takes a whole squad of mentors, editors, marketers, and encouragers to reach the destination of publication.

I'm so grateful to:

ALISON BEHNKE. Your blend of constructive and positive feedback has simultaneously stretched and emboldened me. As a somewhat new writer who sometimes lacks confidence, I honestly believe God gifted me with the perfect editor for this piece. You've been kind, reflective, and enlightening throughout the process, and I'm not sure I would have made it through without you.

CORY THOMAS. You, sir, are a highly talented artist. Your illustrations create a vibrant, intriguing appeal for young readers. Teens struggling will flip through these pages. As they do, your engaging art will leave an impression on their hearts much more profound than my words ever could.

AMANDA SHOFNER. You've been the steady go-to the whole time I've worked with Free Spirit. You've been responsive and supportive when I needed help with orders, marketing, blogging, speaking, and publishing. You are a gem for the company, and it's been an honor to work with you over the years.

COURTENAY FLETCHER. You've laid the groundwork for a design that will vibe with teens. I can't imagine how much time and energy it took to design the chapter openers, folios, and fonts—not to mention typesetting the entire book. You are a true visionary. Thanks for your expertise and dedication.

ALYSSA LOCHNER. Because of you, the text is clear, consistent, and reader-friendly. Your disciplined attention to detail—from the technical stuff like grammar and formatting, to higher-level considerations like word choice, transitions, and style—is next level. I appreciate you crossing all our i's and dotting all our t's.

CHET WILLIAMS AND TRENT MORROW. You are the two sages of my adulthood. After I committed myself to rehab a few years ago, I needed one skilled therapist to rekindle my fire for existence. I consider it a great fortune to have found two. Your wisdom in the realms of CBT and REBT brought light to a dark path that I will carry with me throughout my journey. You helped me defeat my demons. Because of you, I can help teens bury their demons too.

SAMANTHA ASHLEY, ROB BAILEY, ERICA GILES, GRACYN CHEYNEY, AND MICHELLE RUSGO. I can't thank you enough for listening to me babble on and on about chapter ideas and for helping me come up with fresh, new content. I'm blessed to have a dedicated wife and best friends who invested heavily in this project.

BRIAN SLATTERY. You are the quintessential servant-leader, a principal that many teachers can only dream of having. I love how you constantly check in to see how my students and I are doing, give me grace on my bad days, advocate for me behind closed doors, and speak to the better angels of my nature. I don't want to quit teaching, but I've also had this dream deep in my spirit to pen a book for teens. Instead of asking me to make a fork-in-the-road decision, you've helped me find a path forward where both passions merged into one.

ANNE DEVLIN. Years ago, I found myself defeated, sitting with my MacBook, reading email replies from dozens of literary agents telling me "No," that I didn't have a book in me. Then I read your email, which was the "Yes" I needed. Together, we provided a helping hand to thousands of burnt-out teachers with *The Balanced Teacher Path,* and I hope we will guide as many teens through this second work. I'm indebted for your *yes* in a world full of *no's.*

RECOMMENDED RESOURCES

Books

The Anti-Anxiety Notebook: Cognitive Behavioral Therapy and Other Essentials, edited by Hod Tamir, Rachel E. Brenner, Diana Hu, Emory Strickland, and Haley Nahman (New York: Therapy Notebooks, 2020).

Boy Meets Depression: Or Life Sucks and Then You Live, by Kevin Breel (New York: Harmony Books, 2015).

The Dream Interpretation Handbook: A Guide and Dictionary to Unlock the Meanings of Your Dreams, by Karen Frazier (Emeryville, CA: Althea Press, 2019).

Happier, No Matter What: Cultivating Hope, Resilience, and Purpose in Hard Times, by Tal Ben-Shahar (New York: The Experiment, 2021).

The Little Book of Hygge: Danish Secrets to Happy Living, by Meik Wiking (New York: William Morrow, 2017).

The Obstacle Is the Way: The Timeless Art of Turning Trials into Triumph, by Ryan Holiday (New York: Portfolio/Penguin, 2014).

The Scandinavian Guide to Happiness: The Nordic Art of Happy and Balanced Living with Fika, Lagom, Hygge, and More, by Tim Rayborn (Kennebunkport, Me: Whalen Book Works, 2021).

Sleep Smarter: 21 Essential Strategies to Sleep Your Way to a Better Body, Better Health, and Bigger Success, by Shawn Stevenson (New York: Rodale Books, 2016).

Why We Sleep: Unlocking the Power of Sleep and Dreams, by Matthew Walker (New York: Scribner, 2017).

The Wisdom of No Escape and the Path of Loving-Kindness, by Pema Chödrön (New York: Random House, 2018).

Online Resources

The Daily Stoic: Ancient Wisdom for Everyday Life, dailystoic.com.

"Multiple Intelligence Assessment—Find Your Strengths!" literacynet.org/mi/assessment/findyourstrengths.html.

"Social Media & Screen Addiction," Calm Masterclass by Dr. Adam Alter, calm.com/app/program/VkZ7_y1PV.

"Universal Emotions," by Paul Ekman, paulekman.com/universal-emotions.

"Writing and Performing Poetry," MasterClass by Amanda Gorman (2022), masterclass.com/classes/amanda-gorman-teaches-writing-and-performing-poetry.

INDEX

ABOUT THE AUTHOR AND ILLUSTRATOR

Justin Ashley is a nationally recognized, award-winning teacher, published author, work-life balance coach, and motivational speaker from Charlotte, North Carolina, where he began teaching in 2007.

He has taught for 15 years in Charlotte-Mecklenburg Schools. He earned his undergraduate education degree as an NC Teaching Fellows Scholar at UNC Charlotte and also holds a master's degree in educational leadership from Wingate University.

In 2011, Justin was named the Charlotte-Mecklenburg Schools East Zone Teacher of the Year and in 2013, he became the only teacher to ever win 2 state titles—the North Carolina History Teacher of the Year and North Carolina Social Studies Teacher of the Year—in the same year.

Most importantly, Justin is a proud husband to his wonderful wife, Samantha, and a dedicated father to his two amazing kids, Cole and Savannah. He enjoys playing basketball with his son, singing all things Disney with his daughter, and nature walking with his wife. His favorite family vacation spots in North Carolina are Wilmington and Asheville.

Cory Thomas is a Trinidad-born illustrator, writer, and interesting man. As a kid, his artistic abilities began to manifest themselves through his majestic stick figures and exquisite scribbling. Substituting comic books for friends, he developed an interest in art and quickly became one of the preeminent six-year-olds in his field. In 2005 he began the newspaper comic strip Watch Your Head and in 2013 began his journey into middle-grade literature. Cory now lives in Atlanta, Georgia, with his wife, Netflix, and too many hats.